MW00424025

"In *The Covenantal [Life]*
to build up the bo[dy]
Bible study, biblic[al] intent is to provide the reader with a clear picture of the big story of Scripture and the implications of that story for the lives of professing believers. Sarah provides more than just information to stimulate your thinking; she challenges readers to live out the doctrine of Scripture in a way that demonstrates the genuine community found in the body of Christ. This book would be valuable to any group or church that desires to build a community of love on a solid biblical foundation."

—Stephen Estock, Coordinator, PCA Discipleship Ministries

"*The Covenantal Life* adorns the multifaceted splendor of covenant theology and covenant life. This resource is designed to help women think biblically and live covenant-ally. I heartily recommend this covenant primer because it makes these doctrines accessible and easily transferable."

—Karen Hodge, Women's Ministry Coordinator for the
PCA and author of *Transformed: Life-Taker to Life-Giver*

"I'm staring at my office bookshelves and noticing that I do not have one book about covenant theology written by a woman. Leave it to Sarah Ivill to be the first to write one. Sarah's *The Covenantal Life* is clear and compelling, and it reignited my love for the beauty of Christ seen in covenant theology. Not only does it give us a thorough understanding of covenant theology but even more, it gives us a practical look at how this truth works itself out at the street level of our lives. This is required reading for all women leading a Bible study or small group who long to see Christ in all of the Bible as they disciple others."

—Kari Stainback, Director of Women's Ministries,
Park Cities Presbyterian Church

"Covenant theology and covenant community are insepa-rable. Our theology explains who God is, who we are, and why we do what we do; and our communal life demon-strates in live action what we believe. There is a beautiful unity that flows from theology to life, and that's because God is the progenitor of both. As Christians, we show the world that we love because He first loved us. Sarah Ivill puts it all together for us in this accessible study. Thank you, Sarah. If you are a Bible teacher in your church, if you want to be grounded in the truth, if you want to train oth-ers to know and love and teach the Bible, then you will be grateful to Sarah for providing in this book the foundation for understanding the connecting threads of the theology of the Bible and biblical living that flows from it. In this volume she rightly joins theology and life to show the unde-niable truth that how we think determines how we act."

—Donna Dobbs, Director of Christian Education,
First Presbyterian Church, Jackson, Mississippi

"As a former attorney and a professional mediator for over twenty years, I have enjoyed many resources that help people to strengthen and enjoy community. As a seminary student, I delight in books that elucidate both philosophy and theology, especially covenant theology. But this *tour de force* from Sarah Ivill is the first book I have endorsed that perfectly illumines the way that 'covenant theology leads to community life that is governed by the God of the covenant.' As you study this resource alone or in groups, I am confident that you will be well grounded in truth and then equipped to graciously share that truth with others because 'theology is not just something we know; it is also something we do.' Is the community of your church a bit anemic? Read this book. Are you looking for a biblically rich but accessible book to review the key tenants of cov-enant theology? Read this book. And would you like to know how to identify your spiritual gifts so that you can serve your covenant community? Sarah Ivill has provided the just-right book for you! *The Covenantal Life* grounds us in the truth of Scripture. *The Covenantal Life* equips us to keep an eternal perspective. In *The Covenantal Life*, Sarah Ivill brings scholarship and relationship together in life-giving, encouraging, equipping ways. I heartily recommend this book."

—Tara Barthel, author and mediator

"With biblical clarity and warm insights, Sarah Ivill invites us to worship and to grow in our understanding of who God is and who we are as His people. For many it will be a joyous rehearsal as we meet afresh the God of steadfast love and faithfulness. Others will grasp in a richer depth who and what the God of covenant faithfulness has done in and for them. May this study call us to worship, rejoice in our God, and commit to life-giving kingdom service."

—Jane Patete, former Coordinator of Women's Ministry—
The Presbyterian Church in America

"Sarah has written a book that joins two of my favorite church loves—covenant and community. Believers need to know the *why* before they can appreciate the *how* to live. This book simply presents the why and the how, but most of all for Whom we live and love."

—Susan Tyner, Coordinator of Women's Ministry,
Christ Presbyterian Church, Oxford, Mississippi,
and PCA Women's Ministry Regional Advisor

The Covenantal Life

The Covenantal Life

Appreciating the Beauty of Theology and Community

Sarah Ivill

Reformation Heritage Books
Grand Rapids, Michigan

The Covenantal Life
© 2018 by Sarah Ivill

Reformation Heritage Books
2965 Leonard St. NE
Grand Rapids, MI 49525
616-977-0889
orders@heritagebooks.org
www.heritagebooks.org

Scripture taken from the New King James Version®. Copyright © 1982 by Thomas Nelson. Used by permission. All rights reserved.

Printed in the United States of America
18 19 20 21 22 23/10 9 8 7 6 5 4 3 2 1

Library of Congress Cataloging-in-Publication Data

Names: Ivill, Sarah, author.
Title: The covenantal life : appreciating the beauty of theology and
    community / Sarah Ivill.
Description: Grand Rapids, Michigan : Reformation Heritage
    Books, 2018.
Identifiers: LCCN 2017058508 (print) | LCCN 2017060775 (ebook)
    | ISBN 9781601785930 (epub) | ISBN 9781601785923 (pbk. : alk.
    paper)
Subjects: LCSH: Reformed Church—Doctrines. | Covenant theology.
Classification: LCC BX9422.3 (ebook) | LCC BX9422.3 .I95 2018
    (print) | DDC 230/.51—dc23
LC record available at https://lccn.loc.gov/2017058508

*For additional Reformed literature, request a free book list from
Reformation Heritage Books at the above regular or e-mail address.*

To the Covenant King and Covenant Keeper, Jesus Christ,
and to His bride, the covenant community,
especially my sisters at Christ Covenant Church

Contents

Foreword

I know Sarah personally. That always makes a difference when picking up a book. Reading through these
pages, I can recognize her personality, hear her tone,
and track with her heart. As Sarah's pastor and friend,
I can tell you she is as genuine as they come. She takes
Bible study and writing as seriously as any layperson I
know. It's no wonder her classes for women at Christ
Covenant are usually packed out. She has a hunger for
God's Word and a passion for other women to see the
riches of the Bible for themselves.

But more important than Sarah being someone
you would like, the content in this book is truth you
should like. If you are from a Presbyterian or Reformed
background, you may be tired of hearing about the
covenants. And if you are from a different church tradition, you may not have heard much about "covenant" at
all. In either case, don't let the title scare you off. Yes,
this is a book about the covenantal life. But that's just
another way of saying this is a book about the Christian
life. Our God is a God who establishes relationship with
His people, a relationship rooted in covenant patterns

and covenant promises. To be a Christian is to worship a covenant-keeping God, to dwell in covenant community, and to partake of the new covenant meal of bread and cup.

The Covenantal Life is a great resource for introducing (or reaffirming) these truths. Sarah writes clearly and carefully, with important lessons drawn from the Bible and the confessions of the church (and good alliteration to boot!). She focuses on The Story, but she's not afraid to share her own stories as well. Women will find Sarah to be a sure guide in our confusing cultural moment. And just as crucially, they will find the covenantal life to be God's best for them now and forever.

Kevin DeYoung
Senior Pastor
Christ Covenant Church
Matthews, North Carolina

A Note from Sarah

We are living in a day when many of us have lost our appreciation for the beauty of covenant theology. This has had dire consequences. Much of the church has traded in a God-centered theology for a self-centered one. Many believers have exchanged Bible studies for book studies. They have exalted heroes of the faith more than the Hero of the faith, Jesus Christ. They have exchanged God's promises and freedom for the world's promises and enslavement. And they have forgotten the doctrines of grace, thinking they are pretty good people who can earn God's favor, that there are many ways to heaven, that God's grace is license to sin, and that they are capable of preserving their destinies.

We are also living in a day when many of us have lost our appreciation for the beauty of covenant community. And this too has had dire consequences. Many believers have traded in interdependence in the community of grace for individualism and isolationism. They have exchanged biblical womanhood for feminism. They have taken liberty to speak whatever is on their mind instead of speaking the truth in love. They

have forgotten their mission, thinking their life plans
and dreams are for their own choosing and glory. And
they have forgotten their destination, failing to live with
an eternal perspective.

It is my conviction that a key solution to this problem
is a return to a robust knowledge of Reformed theology,
which, rightly understood, is covenant theology. Such a
robust understanding of covenant theology should in turn
lead to a rich engagement with the covenant community.

Covenant theology is not a system of doctrine
imposed on Scripture; rather, it is God's own way of
speaking about the gospel in all the Scripture, from
Genesis to Revelation. Therefore, knowledge of covenant theology deepens our knowledge and appreciation
of the only true God and Jesus Christ, whom He sent,
and our relationship to one another as the people of
God—the covenant community.

Covenant theology deepened my appreciation for
Jesus's life, death, resurrection, and ascension. It heightened my appreciation for all the spiritual blessings I
have in Christ. It broadened my appreciation of the sacraments, baptism and the Lord's Supper. It deepened
my sense of wonder at how God's sovereignty and my
responsibility go hand in hand. And it heightened my
appreciation of how Scripture fit together as one big
covenant story stretching from Genesis to Revelation,
with Christ as the center of it all. In turn, it deepened
my appreciation and love for the covenant community,
heightened my awareness of my design as a woman,
broadened my love for multigenerational ministry,
helped me understand how the cultural mandate and

the Great Commission go hand in hand, and filled me with hope for the city that is to come.

For this reason, my prayer for you as you read this book is the same as Paul's prayer for the saints who were in Ephesus:

> that He would grant you, according to the riches of His glory, to be strengthened with might through His Spirit in the inner man, that Christ may dwell in your hearts through faith; that you, being rooted and grounded in love, may be able to comprehend with all the saints what is the width and length and depth and height—to know the love of Christ which passes knowledge; that you may be filled with all the fullness of God. (Eph. 3:16–19)

Soli Deo gloria!

Acknowledgments

I want to thank those in my life who have been a part of this writing process.

Thank you to Reformation Heritage Books, especially Jay Collier, for initiating this process and to Annette Gysen for her excellent editorial work.

Thank you to Jane Patete, former women's ministry coordinator for the Presbyterian Church in America (PCA), who first encouraged me to publish this material.

Thank you to Karen Hodge, women's ministry coordinator for the PCA, as well as Stephen Estock, coordinator for the PCA Discipleship Ministries, who read through an early version of this manuscript and gave me valuable feedback.

Thank you to my pastor, Kevin DeYoung, for writing the foreword, as well as to the women's ministry leadership at Christ Covenant Church for asking me to teach a women's class on this material, and to the women in the class who encouraged and supported this project.

Thank you to Westminster Theological Seminary for the many online class lectures, chapel messages, and books that I have benefited from, which have taught me what it means to see Christ in all of Scripture and to understand more deeply the history of redemption and the beautiful truths of Reformed theology.

Thank you to Reformed Theological Seminary, for the many online classes I have benefited from, especially the class on covenant theology taught by Ligon Duncan.

Thank you to my parents, David and Judy Gelaude, who have always encouraged me to continue in the work of the Lord.

Thank you to my husband, Charles, who once again gave me his loyal support in the publishing process and who prayed for me and encouraged me as I wrote, and to our children, Caleb, Hannah, Daniel, and Lydia, who are a constant source of encouragement to me as I pray for the next generation of believers to love the Lord and His people.

Finally, thank you to my heavenly Father, to my Lord and Savior Jesus Christ, and to the Spirit, who helps me in my weakness. To the triune God be the glory for what He has done through me, a broken vessel and a flawed instrument, yet one that is in the grip of His mighty and gracious hand.

Introduction

Over the years I have been serving in women's ministry, I have had the privilege of counseling, teaching, and praying for many women—single women who longed to be married, married women who experienced the pain that comes with infidelity, mothers who grieved over a child who chose to live an ungodly lifestyle, daughters who experienced the stress of caring for aging parents, mothers who have struggled to walk away from a career to raise children or struggled to walk away from home to begin a career, women who suffered the painful journey of infertility or miscarriages, and women who couldn't shake the shame they felt over sexual sin.

These are not just women I have had the privilege to know, though; they are women you know too. They are women who sit beside us in the church pew or next to us in Bible study, or maybe they sing alongside us in the choir. They are sisters in Christ who often cry out for help through a conversation, text, email, or phone call, wondering if and how we will respond. Or maybe one of these women reminds you of your own circumstances, and you are wondering how to respond to suffering, sin, or shame.

What do we say when our sisters come to us for help? Giving them a hug, taking them a meal, or sending them a note of encouragement is wonderful, but it isn't enough. We must lead them to a person—Jesus Christ. The same is true for us. When we find ourselves in a situation like these women, we must look to Jesus. Without a robust view of our Redeemer, we are all likely to revel in our sin, remain in our shame, retreat into our suffering, or run ashore in our service.

We must first learn how to think theologically when the storms of life come our way (suffering), when shame closes in around us (sin), and when we seek to serve the triune God in the midst of a fallen world (service)—and then help our sisters learn how. In other words, we must all be good theologians. This means we must have sound doctrine to interpret our life events and to help one another live accordingly.

It is instructive that when Paul wrote to the Galatians about a particular problem (they were turning to a different gospel), he began with, "Grace to you and peace from God the Father and our Lord Jesus Christ, who gave Himself for our sins, that He might deliver us from this present evil age, according to the will of our God and Father, to whom be glory forever and ever. Amen" (Gal. 1:3–5). In other words, Paul began with the person who could solve their problems. He wasn't leading people through a ten-step program but to the person and work of Jesus Christ. He painted a robust picture of redemption as a backdrop for calling God's people to repentance and renewal. As we journey through our own suffering, sin, and service, and as we help our sisters through theirs, we must do the same.

I have divided this book on the covenantal life into two parts: "Appreciating the Beauty of Covenant Theology" and "Appreciating the Beauty of Covenant Community." After reading each chapter, you will have the opportunity under the "Thinking It Through" section to apply the truths you have learned to your present suffering, sin, and service so that you can better apply covenant theology to all of life, especially as it applies to life in the covenant community. I urge you to take the time to do this. It will bear much fruit if you apply what you are learning to your specific circumstances.

If you are studying this book with a group, I encourage you to be willing to share your answers and applications with your sisters so that you might comfort one another in your sufferings, challenge one another to repent of your sins, and strengthen one another as you serve Christ and His church. My hope and prayer is that you will come away with a deeper knowledge and appreciation of the only true God and Jesus Christ, whom He sent, and of our relationship to one another as sisters in Christ.

Part 1

Appreciating the Beauty
of Covenant Theology

Chapter 1

Better Promises

The day of my wedding, I was so nervous I thought I was going to be sick. I wasn't nervous about marrying my husband but about singing in front of all the wedding guests. What was even more nerve-wracking was that my solo was a surprise. What would my soon-to-be-husband do when I suddenly pulled out a microphone and started singing "I Will Be Here" to him? Even worse, what would I do? Would I be able to make it through the song without crying? Would he? I started having serious doubts that a surprise solo was a good idea. Nevertheless, before the ceremony was over, I had surprised my husband with a solo at our wedding—and the guests too!

The song I sang is rightly titled "I Will Be Here." I repeated the phrase twelve times before my solo was over, reiterating that through darkness, cold feelings, swings of emotions, an unclear future, and an aging body, I would remain faithful to my husband, for good or for bad, for richer or for poorer, in sickness and in health, until we are parted by death.

As wonderful a day as my wedding was and as solemn as my vows were, the story of my covenant marriage pales in comparison to another bride and groom and wedding that is enacted on better promises. In this chapter I want to tell you about Someone who has made a promise to be here for us, whether we are naughty or nice, dressed in robes or rags, or are strong or sick. I want to tell you about the covenant-keeping God.

What Is God?
In answer 7, the Westminster Larger Catechism (WLC) tells us that "God is a Spirit, in and of himself infinite in being, glory, blessedness, and perfection; all-sufficient, eternal, unchangeable, incomprehensible, every where present, almighty, knowing all things, most wise, most holy, most just, most merciful and gracious, long-suffering, and abundant in goodness and truth."

Don't rush past this definition. Today, many people have brought God down to a level they can understand. For example, I have heard people refer to God as the daddy upstairs (in heaven). Or they think of God like they do Santa Claus, believing He brings gifts according to whether they've been naughty or nice. Or they treat God as they do a doctor; they go to Him only when they are in dire circumstances. But infinite in glory? Incomprehensible? Almighty? Most holy? Most merciful and gracious? These aren't usually the words on people's lips when they are asked, "What is God?"

Scripture reveals to us that this one true God is triune—one God existing in three persons, the Father, the Son, and the Holy Spirit. He is sovereign over all things and is providentially bringing His plans and purposes to pass.

It is amazing news that we serve a triune God who in and of Himself is infinite in being, all-sufficient, almighty, most merciful and gracious, and abundant in goodness and truth. Even more amazing is that He created us to glorify and enjoy Him forever. Stop and ponder that for a moment. Why would the Creator God want us to be in such a relationship with Him that we could actually enjoy Him? And how can we even have such a relationship with Him when there is a huge difference and distance between the Creator and His creatures, so great that there is no way we could possibly bridge it? To be sure, we are responsible to obey Him as our Creator, but to enjoy a relationship with Him and all the blessings such a relationship brings? We could never do that if He didn't intervene. It is incredible to learn, then, that God has bridged the gap for us. He voluntarily agreed to come and initiate a relationship with us. This relationship is displayed by way of covenant, a concept we will keep returning to in this book.

What Is Covenant?
A thorough yet concise definition of covenant is *God's sovereign initiation to have a binding relationship with His people, grounded in His grace and promises, and secured by His own blood.* It might be helpful for you to think of four *P*'s when you are trying to grasp the word *covenant* according to the entirety of Scripture. These four *P*'s will also help you understand how the Old Testament and New Testament fit together.

The first word to keep in mind is the *promise* of God's presence. Over and over in Scripture you will read the promise, "I will be your God, and you will be My people" (see, for example, Gen. 17:7–8; Ex. 6:7; Lev. 26:12; Jer. 32:38; Ezek. 14:11; Zech. 8:8; 2 Cor. 6:16; Heb. 8:10; Rev. 21:3). When you find it, mark it in red. It will become a beautiful thread running through your Bible, reminding you of God's covenant promise, sealed with His own blood.

Throughout redemptive history we see a progression of God dwelling with His people. First, we observe Him dwelling with Adam and Eve in the garden. He blessed them, gave them His instruction, and confronted them when they disobeyed (Gen. 1:28–30; 2:16–17; 3:8–13, 16–19). Then, after God delivered His people Israel from Egypt, we see Him meet with them in the tabernacle, which was a tent that contained the ark of the covenant with the mercy seat in the Most Holy Place, where the Lord would descend to meet with Moses in order to instruct him in the way He wanted His people to live (Ex. 25:10–22). Moses erected the tabernacle in the first month of the second year after the Lord delivered Israel. The cloud of the Lord was on the tabernacle by day and fire was over it by night in order to lead Israel on their journeys through the wilderness (Ex. 40:16–18, 34–38). Eventually the Lord dwells with His people in the temple. The Lord chose King Solomon to build His temple in Jerusalem. Like the tabernacle, the temple had a Most Holy Place that contained the ark of the covenant where the Lord would meet with His people above the mercy seat (Ex. 25:17–22; 1 Kings 6:1–38; 8:1–11). But the climax of God dwelling with His people is when Jesus came to earth and lived among us, fulfilling God's promise, "I will be your God, and you will be My people." The apostle John puts it this way: "And the Word became flesh and dwelt [literally "tabernacled"] among us, and we beheld His glory, the glory as of the only begotten of the Father, full of grace and truth" (John 1:14). John is helping his readers understand that the true and final tabernacle has come! What the garden, the tabernacle, and the temple prefigured, Christ fulfilled. When Christ returns, He will consummately fulfill this promise as we dwell with the triune God in the new heaven and the new earth forever: "And I heard a loud voice from heaven saying, 'Behold, the tabernacle of God is with men, and He will dwell with them, and they shall be His people. God Himself will be with them and be their God'" (Rev. 21:3).

The second *P* word to remember is the *person* of Jesus Christ. All Scripture points to Christ. The prophets, priests, kings, and sacrifices of the Old Testament foreshadowed the Promised One to come. When the prophets proclaimed the words of God, they anticipated the living Word of God, Christ, who as the final and perfect prophet reveals to us by His Word and Spirit the will of God for our salvation (Westminster Shorter Catechism [WSC], A. 25). When the priests offered up the sacrifices year after year to atone for Israel's sin, they anticipated the final and perfect priest, Jesus Christ, who offered Himself up for us on the cross to satisfy God's divine justice, to reconcile us to God, and to continually intercede for us (WSC, A. 25). When the kings ruled over Israel, fighting their enemies and ruling over the people, they anticipated the final and perfect King, Jesus Christ, who rules and defends us and conquers all His and our enemies (WSC, A. 26). What Augustine said is true: "The New is in the Old concealed; the Old is in the New revealed."

The third *P* word is the *people* of God. Throughout redemptive history we see God choose one man (Adam), then one family (Abraham's), then one nation (Israel), and then, as Ephesians 2:14–16 says, one new man in place of the two, Jews and Gentiles, through the cross (the New Testament church) in order to continue the promised line through which the Promised One, Jesus Christ, would come. We rightly teach our covenant children:

> Father Abraham had many sons,
> Many sons had Father Abraham.
> I am one of them, and so are you.
> So let's all praise the Lord.

There has always been one people of God saved by grace alone through faith alone.

The final word to remember is the *practice* of God's people. The Lord saved Israel out of Egypt and then instructed them how to live. It's important that we get this in the right order! He saved them first and then gave them the Ten Commandments. Because God is the Covenant King, we are to respond to His grace as covenant servants by glorifying Him. We do this by loving Him, trusting Him, enjoying Him, and obeying Him. God's people are to be holy because He is holy and are to proclaim the excellencies of Him who called us out of darkness into light (1 Peter 1:15–16; 2:9–12). Question 32 of the Heidelberg Catechism asks, "Why are you called a Christian," and the answer is, "Because I am a member of Christ by faith and thus share in His anointing so that I may as prophet confess His Name, as priest present myself a living sacrifice of thankfulness to Him, and as king fight with a free and good conscience against sin and the devil in this life, and hereafter reign with Him eternally over all creatures."

It is important to note that the concept of covenant is rooted in the first relationship between God and humankind in the garden of Eden. The Creator God initiated a relationship with His creation from the beginning. He put Adam in the garden and commanded him to live according to His word. He held out a blessing of life for obedience and a curse of death for disobedience: "Of every tree of the garden you may freely eat; but of the tree of the knowledge of good and evil you shall not eat, for in the day that you eat of it you shall surely die" (Gen. 2:16–17).

After Adam and Eve sinned, we see God take the initiative in the relationship that was now broken. He called to them, questioned them, and punished them for disobedience. It is clear that He is king. But there is a gospel note of grace sounded in Genesis 3:15 we shouldn't miss that we will discuss more fully in chapter 3, which anticipates Christ's life, death, resurrection, ascension and return:

> And I will put enmity
> Between you and the woman,
> And between your seed and her Seed;
> He shall bruise your head,
> And you shall bruise His heel.

Self-Centered or God-Centered?

Since the Creator God has voluntarily initiated a relationship with us, we should ask ourselves how often we
delight in God. Do we enjoy praying to Him, reading His
Word, and fellowshipping with His people as much as we
enjoy art, entertainment, food, hiking, reading, or shop-
ping? Because God created us to glorify Him and enjoy
Him forever, it follows that our deepest contentment
is found when He is most glorified in our lives. So why
are we so often drawn to find our contentment in other
things? It happens because our own flesh, the world, and
the devil want us to believe that our deepest contentment is found when we glorify and enjoy ourselves. This
leads us to have a self-centered approach to our life and
faith instead of a God-centered one. For example, notice
the difference in each case between statements A and B:

A. If only I hadn't gotten myself into this mess!

B. The Lord has placed me in this circumstance.
   I wonder what He will teach me through this.

A. When I get done raising these four children, I
   am going to have a little more time to myself!

B. What a privilege it is to train these children for
   the Lord's service. When the years of training
   are over, I will continue the hard work of praying every day that the Lord will use them for
   His kingdom purposes.

A. If I treated my husband the way he treats me, he wouldn't like it one bit. I thought marriage was a 50/50 effort. I am pulling 100 percent.

B. The Lord gave my husband to me because this is who He knew was best for me. I can trust Him to bring good even out of difficult circumstances and to bring glory to His name.

A. I accepted Jesus into my heart.

B. God opened up my blind eyes, unstopped my deaf ears, and softened my hard heart, saving me by His grace alone.

These statements, and others like them, reveal how we think about God—our theology—and this theology affects every area of our lives. In order to have sound theology, we must renew our minds from the ruckus sounds of reckless and wrong theology surrounding us every day. And as I stated in my note at the beginning of this book, it is my conviction that a key solution to reckless and wrong theology is a return to a robust knowledge of Reformed theology, which, rightly understood, is covenant theology.

Theology is not just something we know; it is also something we do. We live out our theology every day. The way we define our purpose in life, the priorities we set, the meaning we assign to events or people, the hope that we have in life circumstances, the explanations that we give for blessings and suffering, and the reaction we have in the face of tragedy and pain convey our theology.

It is important, then, that we have a proper worldview from which to evaluate the events in our lives so that we form right conclusions about God, humanity, and the world around us. And since we are in a covenant relationship with God and with others, it makes sense that we need a covenantal worldview.

A Covenantal Worldview
We must have a worldview that flows from the covenant story of the Bible, which can be summarized in four words: creation, fall, redemption, and restoration. This covenant story, stretching from Genesis to Revelation, is found in seed form in the first three chapters of Genesis. The triune God created the world out of nothing. He created man in His own image, male and female (Gen. 1:27). He initiated a covenantal relationship with the first man and first woman, Adam and Eve, through a covenant of works (we'll learn more about this covenant in chapter 3), which laid out how things should work in His kingdom (Gen. 2:15–17). But Adam and Eve failed to obey God's word and fell into sin and separation from God. True to covenant form, God cursed them for such disobedience, but He also promised a way of reconciliation. One day Someone would come and crush the serpent, freeing humankind from sin and death and reconciling God's people to Him again. These first three chapters of Genesis, as well as the entirety of Scripture, help us understand what it means to have a covenantal worldview through which to interpret our lives.

First, we must view the world in which we live as God's world, created by Him. After He created Adam and Eve on the sixth day, He gave them a mandate that informed their worldview and subsequently informs ours: "Then God blessed them, and God said to them, 'Be fruitful and multiply; fill the earth and subdue it; have dominion over the fish of the sea, over the birds of the air, and over every living thing that moves on the earth'" (Gen. 1:28).

In this verse we see four *W*'s that are important for understanding a covenantal worldview—worship, woman, work, and the Word of God. We will look more closely at these in chapter 9, but for now I want us to see that we are to be worshipers of God grounded in His Word, women who live out their design as life givers (more about this in chapter 7) grounded in His Word, and workers who go into the world grounded in His Word. Also, we should not forget the truth of Genesis 1:31: "Then God saw everything that He had made, and indeed it was very good." The song "This Is My Father's World" should ring in our hearts each day.

Second, we must view the sin and suffering in our lives and in our world as a result of the fall. We must simultaneously remember three things—we are loved by God and called to be saints (Rom. 1:7), we will suffer for Christ's name's sake (Phil. 1:29), and we will continue to sin on this side of glory (Gal. 5:17). We will talk more about these three truths in chapter 8.

Third, we must see our solution as the only Lord and Savior, Jesus Christ. Salvation is of the Lord. Jesus is our Redeemer, freeing us from slavery to sin and death into eternal life with Him. We will look more closely at this solution in chapter 4.

The redeemed have a new mission that goes along with the cultural mandate in Genesis 1. Although we don't leave any of the *W*'s we've already considered behind, we do add one—witness. We are to be witnesses grounded in the Word of God, proclaiming Christ to a lost and dying world (more about this in chapter 9).

Finally, we must await Christ's second coming in hope and anticipation of the consummation of His kingdom, when He will make all things new. Jesus is presently seated at the right hand of God the Father, praying for us and awaiting the day He is charged by His Father to come and take us to our eternal home (Heb. 1:3–4; 4:14–16; 9:24–28).

I'm not sure I would recommend singing a surprise solo at your wedding, but I do recommend singing each day about the One who has made a covenant promise to be here for you. He loved you even when you were a covenant breaker. And He has reconciled you to Himself through His Son, the perfect Covenant Keeper, who is coming again to take you home to be with the triune God for all eternity. Now that's something to sing about!

Thinking It Through

- Jot down your present sin, suffering, and service in light of what you have learned about God, the covenant, and a covenantal worldview in this chapter.

Sin—

Suffering—

Service—

• Spend time in thanksgiving today that the triune God has voluntarily initiated a relationship
  with you expressed by way of covenant.

• In what people, places, or things do you seek
  comfort? How has this chapter challenged you
  to find your deepest contentment in Christ?

• Would you say your thoughts are more God-
  centered or self-centered? Why?

• In what present circumstance would applying a
  covenantal worldview help you think through
  things clearly?

Chapter 2

The Best Book Ever

One of my favorite books I have read aloud to my children, which is also one of the hardest to read (I always seem to end up in tears), is *The Hiding Place*, the story of Corrie Ten Boom. During World War II in the Netherlands, Corrie spent time in prison and in a concentration camp for her unswerving efforts to help persecuted Jews. Her story recounts the events that led to her imprisonment, her time in prison, and her life after she was released when the war was over. One theme that pervades the entire book is her love for the Word of God. It is evident that Corrie, as well as her sister, Betsie, learned this love for Scripture from their father, who routinely held family devotions to impart truth to the next generation and lived his life on the basis of its truth. It was the Word that got the Ten Boom family through horrific circumstances. And it was the Word that changed people's lives around them as they shared the gospel with them.

Their story is a clear example of the truth Moses spoke to Israel: "Set your hearts on all the words which I testify among you today, which you shall command your children to be careful to observe—all the words of this law. For it is not a futile thing for you, *because it is your life*, and by this word you shall prolong your days in the land which you cross over the Jordan to possess" (Deut. 32:46–47, italics mine). During the sisters' stay in Ravensbruck, the women's extermination camp in Germany that had a reputation for its severity, they lived on the words of life. One day, when Corrie didn't think they could possibly live in a flea-infested place any longer, Betsie kept bringing her back to the Scriptures that they read so often, urging her that the way to live in their present circumstances was found in God's Word, and particularly in the passage they had read that morning: "'Rejoice always, pray constantly, give thanks in all circumstances; for this is the will of God in Christ Jesus'—That's it, Corrie! That's His answer. 'Give thanks in all circumstances!' That's what we can do. We can start right now to thank God for every single thing about this new barracks!"[1]

Like Corrie and Betsie, I want to live my life on the basis of the Word of God. It teaches us who God is (the Covenant King and Covenant Keeper), who we are (covenant servants and covenant breakers) and the solution to our problem (Jesus Christ, the Lord of the covenant and the servant of the covenant).

A Covenant Book

In the last chapter we learned that God has initiated a relationship with His people expressed by way of

---

1. Corrie Ten Boom and John and Elizabeth Sherrill, *The Hiding Place* (New York: Bantam Books, 1971), 198.

covenant. In this chapter we will learn that He has graciously chosen to reveal Himself and His will to His people through a covenant book—the written words of Scripture that reveal God's covenantal dealings with His people. That the Creator of the world has chosen to condescend to His people within the context of a covenantal relationship is astounding and glorious news. The Creator King could have chosen to rule His people in another way, but Scripture clearly testifies of His lovingkindness, by which He draws near to His people, declaring the precious promise "I will be your God, and you will be My people" throughout the entire Bible. Also astounding is that the Creator King would give us His Word so that His truth might be preserved and proclaimed and so that the church might be established against the threats of our own flesh, the world, and the devil (Westminster Confession of Faith [WCF], 1.1).

To help us better understand the Bible as a covenant book, I want to focus on one particular book of the Bible—Deuteronomy. First though, I need to explain a concept we're unfamiliar with today but one that was common during the time Moses wrote the book of Deuteronomy—the second-millennium treaty documents of the Hittites. These treaties were between a suzerain (king) and his vassals (servants). These covenant documents began with a preamble in which the covenant king tells who he is with the purpose of instilling fear and reverence among his covenant servants. Next, there is a historical prologue in which the covenant king reminds his covenant servants about what he has done for them in the past, as well as what he has

done for previous generations and how they had inter-
acted with him as servants. The next part of the treaty
contains the stipulations. This is the longest section, as
it contains the obligations of the servants with regard
to their covenant king, as well as the obligations of the
covenant king with regard to his servants. The next part
of the treaty contains a witness clause in which the king
calls on other gods or parts of nature to bear witness
of his treaty and oath to his servants. Next, the treaty
consists of sanctions in which the king lists blessings for
his servants if they obey and curses for his servants if
they disobey. The king's faithfulness is assumed, so no
sanctions are listed for him. The next part of the treaty
contains a statement of display, which states the oath is
inscribed on a tablet as confirmation of the covenant
in written form. Other elements that may or may not
appear in treaties of the second millennium BC include
a servant's oath of obedience, a ceremony or covenant
ratification ritual, and a written procedure as to what to
do in the case of rebellious servants.[2]

So how do these Hittite treaties relate to Deuteronomy and, even more broadly, Scripture as a whole?
Deuteronomy is patterned after the Hittite treaties of
the second millennium BC. The Covenant King, the
Lord God Himself, establishes a treaty with His covenant
people. We could outline the book this way:

---

2. I am indebted to John D. Currid for this information on Hit-
tite treaties. See his commentary for further details: John D. Currid,
A Study Commentary on Deuteronomy, EP Study Commentary (Webster,
N.Y.: Evangelical Press, 2006), 14–16.

The Covenant Speaker (Deut. 1:1–5)
The Covenant Story (Deut. 1:6–4:43)
The Covenant Stipulations (Deut. 4:44–26:19)
   General Stipulations (Deut. 4:44–11:32)
   Specific Stipulations (Deut. 12:1–26:19)
The Covenant Sanctions (Deut. 27:1–30:20)
The Covenant Succession (Deut. 31–34)

You might already be connecting the dots to the entirety of Scripture. The covenant speaker is God Himself, who condescends to people by way of covenant and gives us His Word by which to know Him and live in relationship with Him. The covenant story is, in broad terms, creation, the fall, redemption, and restoration. The covenant stipulations are all the duties the covenant God requires of His covenant people revealed to us in His Word. The covenant sanctions are the blessings for obedience and curses for disobedience recorded in Scripture. As we study the covenant book, it will become clear that we are covenant breakers who deserve God's wrath and curse. The good news of the gospel is that Jesus Christ, the superior mediator to Moses, has come as both Lord of the covenant and servant of the covenant, keeping the covenant perfectly on our behalf and dying a cursed death in our place. All who are in Christ, the Covenant Keeper, stand before the Covenant King robed in Christ's righteousness and fully reconciled to Him.

The Best Book

The Westminster Larger Catechism explains in answer 4 that "the Scriptures manifest themselves to be the Word of God, by their majesty and purity; by the consent of all the parts, and the scope of the whole, which is to give all glory to God; by their light and power to convince and convert sinners, to comfort and build up believers unto salvation." Let's unpack this answer a little bit to better understand how the Scriptures reveal themselves to be God's Word.

First, the Bible reveals itself to be God's word by its "majesty and purity." Since God Himself is majestic, greater than all other names, His word is also majestic, greater than all other words. The psalmist says, "Open my eyes, that I may see wondrous things from Your law" (Ps. 119:18). God's word is also pure. The psalmist tells us,

> The words of the LORD are pure words,
> Like silver tried in a furnace of earth,
> Purified seven times. (Ps. 12:6)

And, "the commandment of the LORD is pure, enlightening the eyes" (Ps. 19:8).

Second, the Bible reveals itself to "be the Word of God…by the consent of all the parts, and the scope of the whole, which is to give all glory to God." Jesus told the Jews, "You search the Scriptures, for in them you think you have eternal life; and these are they which testify of Me" (John 5:39). It is Christ who is the climax of the covenant story and who is testified about on every page of the Bible. As the Covenant King who comes extending grace and mercy, as well as the Covenant Servant to perfectly obey what God's people failed to obey and die a cursed death in their place, He holds the covenant story together as the hero of it all.

Third, the Scriptures reveal themselves to be God's word "by their light and power to convince and convert sinners, to comfort and build up believers unto salvation." Psalm 19:7 says, "The law of the LORD is perfect, converting the soul; the testimony of the LORD is sure, making wise the simple." Paul wrote to the church in Rome, "For whatever things were written before were written for our learning, that we through the patience and comfort of the Scriptures might have hope" (Rom. 15:4). And he commends the elders of the church in Ephesus "to God and to the word of His grace, which is able to build you up and give you an inheritance among all those who are sanctified" (Acts 20:32).

In seminary, I had a dear friend from Ukraine whose conversion story illustrates the truth that God's word is able to convince and convert sinners. She and her twin sister were living in Ukraine and heard that the Navigators were holding a meeting near them. Since they wanted to learn English better, they decided to go and hear the English-speaking people. Soon they became good friends with many of the Navigators. My friend and her sister felt sorry for the Navigators for believing a lie like Christianity and wanted to save them from such wrong beliefs. They began reading the Scriptures so that they could teach their new friends all the errors. But as they studied the Scriptures, the Lord opened *their* blind eyes and saved *them*. The word of God is powerful to convince and convert sinners indeed!

A Different Kind of Book

The apostle Paul tells Timothy that "all Scripture is given by inspiration of God, and is profitable for doctrine, for reproof, for correction, for instruction in righteousness, that the man of God may be complete, thoroughly equipped for every good work" (2 Tim. 3:16–17). These verses teach us several important truths. First, the Bible is different from any other book because God gave it to humankind in order to reveal Himself, and He inspired the human authors as they wrote each of the sixty-six books. Peter says it this way: "No prophecy of Scripture is of any private interpretation, for prophecy never came by the will of man, but holy men of God spoke as they were moved by the Holy Spirit" (2 Peter 1:20–21).

Second, the Word of God is profitable. It will bring forth fruit in our lives. It gives us sound doctrine. It reproves us like a mother reproves a child who has been disobedient. It corrects us like a mother corrects her children when they are in need of training. And it instructs us in righteousness, teaching us the right way to walk—in the fear of the Lord.

Finally, Scripture sanctifies us and equips us to do the work of the Lord. Every good employer has an employee handbook. Scripture is our divine handbook for our work as God's people. It informs us of the when, why, where, what, and how of kingdom worship, kingdom work, and kingdom witness, which we will take a closer look at in chapter 9.

Although I have never experienced the horrific circumstances that Corrie Ten Boom experienced, I do share her love for God's Word. It has gotten me through the deepest waters of suffering, the darkest night of sin and shame, and the toughest seasons of ministry. I hope and pray that you will hold on to it as tightly as you would hold on to a lifeboat in the midst of a raging storm, storing it in your heart for the day you face the storms of suffering, sin, shame, and difficult service.

Thinking It Through

- Jot down your present sin, suffering, and service in light of what you have learned about God's covenant book in this chapter.

  Sin—

  Suffering—

  Service—

- How have you recognized that Scripture alone teaches us what we are to believe about God and how we are to live in relation to Him? How does your life reflect this high view of Scripture?

- What plan do you have to consistently study Scripture, verse by verse, book by book, both individually and corporately?

Chapter 3

The Heart of the Matter

I can still remember my little copy of the Westminster Shorter Catechism that I took to Sunday school at First Associate Reformed Presbyterian Church in Gastonia, North Carolina, where my parents were members during my preschool and early elementary school years. I don't remember the details of the class, but I'm sure we had to learn those questions or I wouldn't have been required to take my copy each week. As I catechize my children, I'm so grateful for the framework that was given to me on which to hang foundational truths of the faith. I couldn't comprehend everything I was learning about covenant theology then, nor can I comprehend it all now, but it gave me a framework for understanding God, His Word, and the significance of Christ's life, death, resurrection, and ascension. I hope and pray I'm giving that same framework to my children, teaching them truth that they will hopefully return to again and again when they battle sin, walk through suffering, or engage in service.[1]

---

1. If you want to catechize your children, I recommend

I want to emphasize the word *framework* because one of the distinctions of covenant theology is interpreting Scripture through a covenantal framework. The covenants structure everything in Scripture and are imperative to a correct understanding of who God is, how we interpret His Word, and how we understand the gospel. It is not an interpretive grid that we impose on Scripture, though. Remember our definition: covenant theology is not a system of doctrine imposed on Scripture; rather, it is God's own way of speaking about the gospel in all the Scripture, from Genesis to Revelation. Therefore, knowledge of covenant theology deepens our knowledge and appreciation of the only true God and Jesus Christ, whom He sent, and our relationship to one another as the people of God—the covenant community. This covenantal framework is already woven into Scripture, and as we will learn in this chapter, it emphasizes a redemptive-historical, Christ-centered approach.[2]

Before we get started, it is important to remember a few things we have already covered in this book. In chapter 1 we learned that God has chosen to enter into a covenant relationship with His people. We also saw that it is important to learn the overarching story of Scripture in order to form a covenantal worldview. In chapter 2

beginning with the Westminster Shorter Catechism, the Heidelberg Catechism, or the New City Catechism.

2. I am greatly indebted to Dr. Edmund Clowney (1917–2005), the first president of Westminster Theological Seminary, for helping me understand, through his writings and online lectures, what it means to employ a redemptive-historical, Christ-centered approach to the study of Scripture. Several helpful resources to deepen your understanding of this topic can be found in the bibliography.

we learned that God has given us a covenant book, the Word of God, so that we can know Him and His will. In this chapter we will further unpack what it means that the Bible is a covenant book by looking at key covenants in redemptive history, the covenant story, and how Christ is the center of the covenant story.

Key Covenants in Redemptive History

Covenant of Redemption

In order to understand the overarching story of Scripture, we need to recognize that God initiated different covenants in the history of redemption: the covenant of redemption, the covenant of works, and the covenant of grace. Ephesians 1:4 teaches us that God the Father chose us in Christ before the foundation of the world (see also John 17:1–5), that we should be holy and blameless before Him. Theologians refer to this as the *covenant of redemption.* The Father has purposed our redemption, the Son has accomplished it, and the Holy Spirit applies it.

Covenant of Works

In Genesis 1 and 2 we learn of God's covenant with Adam before the fall. This covenant established a relationship between the Creator and the creature that involved worship (keeping the Sabbath day holy), work (ruling and multiplying), woman (marriage and procreation), and the word of God (God gave Adam a command when He put him in the garden of Eden to work it and keep it. He could eat of any tree in the garden except one, the tree of the knowledge of good and evil. God told Adam that if he ate of that tree, he would die; if he obeyed, he would live). Theologians refer to this prefall covenant with Adam as the *covenant of works* or the *covenant of life.*

Tragically, Adam failed to obey, and all humanity fell with him in this first transgression. But God sounds a note of grace in Genesis 3:15; death will not have the final word. God promises that He will put enmity between the serpent and the woman and between the serpent's offspring and the woman's offspring. The woman's offspring would bruise the serpent's head, and the serpent would bruise His heel.

Covenant of Grace
Genesis 3:15 is the gospel in seed form. Ultimately, the woman's offspring is Christ. Christ defeated sin and death on the cross, triumphing over all His enemies. God promised the woman that she would continue to produce seed, or offspring, the greatest of whom is Christ. But she would also experience the curse of sorrow with regard to children and the curse of struggle with regard to her husband. God promised the man that he would receive sustenance, but he would also experience the curse of sweaty toil and the separation of soul and body in death. Theologians call this postfall covenant the *covenant of grace.* Titus 3:4–7 provides a good summary of this covenant: "But when the kindness and the love of God our Savior toward man appeared, not by works of righteousness which we have done, but according to His mercy He saved us, through the washing of regeneration and renewing of the Holy Spirit, whom He poured out on us abundantly through Jesus Christ our

Savior, that having been justified by His grace we should become heirs according to the hope of eternal life."

The covenant of grace includes God's postfall covenants with Adam (Gen. 3:15), Noah (Gen. 6:17–22; 8:20–22; 9:1–17), Abraham (Gen. 12:1–3; 15:1–21; 17:1–2), Moses (Exodus 19–24; Deuteronomy), and David (2 Samuel 7), as well as the new covenant, all of which are fulfilled in Jesus Christ (Jer. 31:31–34). Let's take a closer look now at each of these covenants, as well as some other important events that were occurring in redemptive history, so that we have a better grasp of the story of salvation.

The Covenant Story

After the note of the gospel of grace is sounded to Adam and Eve in Genesis 3:15, we learn of God's covenant with Noah. The Lord promises that as long as the earth remains, seedtime and harvest, cold and heat, summer and winter, and day and night will continue (Gen. 8:22). This is amazing grace, for it promises that there will be an earth on which the history of salvation will unfold. Just think if there had been no day for Jesus to be born in Bethlehem or to die on the cross!

In Genesis 9, God's covenant with Noah also promises that though the righteous will be saved, the wicked will be judged, a theme that is predominant through all of Scripture (see, for example, Ps. 7:8–11; Isa. 57:20–21; Matt. 13:47–50; John 3:16–18, 36; 1 Cor. 6:9–10; Rev. 20:11–15). God's original purposes of worship, work, and woman in the prefall covenant with Adam are renewed in the context of the history of redemption. God's covenant with Noah can be summarized by the following: God's *glorious grace* alongside His *glorious justice* (Rev. 20:11–15); the *genealogical aspect* of the covenant (God will deal with families, not just individuals [Gen. 17:9–10; Acts 2:39]); the *goodness of life* (Matt. 6:25–34); and the *general grace* extended to all humankind, including the universe (Matt. 5:45). The sign of this covenant, the rainbow, is most appropriate, then, as it shines God's grace in the midst of the cloudy storm of judgment.

In Genesis we learn of God's covenant with Abraham, which is later renewed with Isaac and Jacob. First, God promises His *presence* (Gen. 17:7–8). The crux of the covenant of grace can be summed up in one phrase: "I will walk among you and be your God, and you shall be My people" (Lev. 26:12). Second, God promises Abraham a *people*; God would make him a great nation (Gen. 12:2; 17:4–6). Third, God promises Abraham a *possession*; He would give His people the land of Canaan (Gen. 12:7; 13:14–17; 15:18–21; 17:8). Fourth, God promises Abraham that He has a bigger *purpose* than he could ever imagine. The nation that came through his seed was to point others to the Lord so that all the families of the earth would be blessed (Gen. 12:3).

To truly understand the concept of covenant, we must look at all the covenants together. We should not reduce the covenant concept to one particular covenant in Scripture. We will consider this covenant with Abraham further, however, because it is one of the most helpful illustrations of the concept of covenant in Scripture. Let's take a closer look at what is going on in Genesis 15.

In Genesis 15 the Lord "cut a covenant" with Abraham. This was entirely different from what people mean when they say they "cut a deal" today. The sovereign Lord didn't cut a deal with Abraham at all. Instead, He cut a covenant that He ensured He would keep, even at the cost of shedding His own blood. The passage is mysterious to us today. We don't typically study this passage with a new believer, but as we will see, we really should because it gives us a magnificent understanding of the covenant of grace.

In the midst of promising Abraham His presence, a people, a possession, and a purpose greater than he could imagine, God told Abraham to assemble five animals (a heifer, a goat, a ram, a turtledove, and a pigeon). Abraham had to cut all the animals, except for the birds, in half. He would have been acquainted with such covenant practices and would have known he was responsible to walk through the animals, pledging his obedience to the terms of the covenant and promising that if he didn't fulfill them he would shed his own blood, as he had shed the animals' blood. But Abraham never had to walk through the animals. Instead, the Lord, by way of a smoking oven and burning torch that passed between the pieces, pledged not only to keep His promises to the point of shedding His own blood but also to keep Abraham's promises to the point of shedding His own blood. In other words, this was a completely unilateral covenant.

You are probably already connecting the dots. Since Abraham and his descendants failed to keep the covenant, God did shed His own blood; the blood of Jesus

Christ was shed for our covenant disobedience. What a beautiful picture of the gospel according to Genesis 15!

In Exodus, we learn of God's covenant with Moses, the mediator of the law the Lord gave to Israel, which can be summarily comprehended in the Ten Commandments. This is the beginning of the theocratic nation of Israel.[3] The holy God brought His people out of slavery in Egypt and into a relationship with Him as His servants. As such, they were to be a kingdom of priests and a holy nation (Ex. 19:6). We learn in both Leviticus 26 and Deuteronomy 28 that if they were obedient, they would receive blessings (Lev. 26:1–13; Deut. 28:1–14), but if they were disobedient, they would receive curses (Lev. 26:14–46; Deut. 28:15–68). The greatest of these curses was exile from the land. But even toward the end of Deuteronomy, we see that God made provision for restoration after the exile, which involved the new covenant (Deut. 30:1–10; see also Jer. 31:31–34; Ezek. 37:21, 26).

In fact, Deuteronomy 28 through 30 is the "CliffsNotes" version of the rest of the Old Testament. First comes blessing, climaxing in the reign of King Solomon (1 Kings 8:24). Then come curses, ultimately resulting in exile from the land (2 Chron. 36:17–21). All the prophets refer to the covenant blessings and curses as they prophesy to Israel and Judah, giving them messages of judgment as well as holding out hope. Though the prophets declare that exile is inevitable, they also

---

3. By a theocratic nation, I mean that Israel's earthly kings, priests, and prophets recognized God as the true King and, as such, served to interpret and enforce His laws for the people.

declare God's faithfulness to His covenant, keeping the promise of the new covenant before them.

After Moses died, the Lord raised up Joshua to lead the people into the Promised Land, which was the place where God would dwell with His people in the temple. Up to this point in redemptive history, the garden of Eden and the tabernacle had been the places the Lord had temporarily dwelt with His people. The entire book of Joshua centers on the entry into and conquest of the land. But then Joshua died, and in the book of Judges we see that the people failed to conquer the land as they should have (Judg. 1:27–36). Instead, they did what was right in their own eyes because there was no king in Israel. The books of Judges and Ruth anticipate the beginning of the monarchy in Israel with King Saul and King David.

In 2 Samuel 7, God makes a covenant with David concerning an eternal kingdom with an eternal Davidic king. First, God promises David a *position*, taking him from being the shepherd of sheep to making him a shepherd-king over His people with a great name. Second, God promises David a *place*. Israel would be planted in their own land. Third, God promises David *peace*. In their own place, Israel would have rest from their enemies. Finally, God promises David *progeny*. The Lord would raise up David's offspring and establish his kingdom forever.

The period of the monarchy climaxes in King Solomon, when the promises are fulfilled in Solomon's prayer of dedication (1 Kings 8:24). Sadly, it didn't take long—within Solomon's reign—for the monarchy to take a turn for the worse (1 Kings 11). Following

Solomon's death, the country actually divided into the Northern Kingdom (Israel) and the Southern Kingdom (Judah) in 931 BC (1 Kings 12:16–24).

Elijah and Elisha preached to the Northern Kingdom during this time. Although there were a few good kings, the majority of kings in both Israel and Judah did evil in the sight of the Lord and led the people into rebellion as well. In His grace and mercy, God raised up prophets during this time to prophesy to the people of coming judgment so that they would turn and repent of their wicked ways. Hosea and Amos preached to the Northern Kingdom while Isaiah and Micah preached to the Southern Kingdom. Joel, Obadiah, and Jonah also preached their messages during this time. Tragically, the Northern Kingdom did not listen and was taken into captivity by the Assyrians in 722 BC.

A little over one hundred years later, the same thing happened to the Southern Kingdom, except it was the Babylonians who took them into captivity. This involved three different deportations in 605, 597, and 586 BC. In the second of these deportations, Jehoiachin, the last, true Davidic king on the throne, was taken, along with the royal family and all the leading classes in Israel, to Babylon. God's promises seemed to be thwarted.

But again, in God's mercy, He raised up both Daniel and Ezekiel to prophesy to the people during the exile (Jeremiah was still prophesying during this time as well). Daniel and Ezekiel spoke messages of both judgment and restoration to the exiles. God would still be faithful to His covenant promise; He would be their God, and they would be His people. Both Jeremiah and Ezekiel spoke of the promised new covenant (Jer. 31:31–34; Ezek. 37:21, 26), which Christ inaugurated during the last Passover (which was also the first Lord's Supper) He celebrated with His disciples before His death.

The new covenant involved seven different promises. First, God promised His people would *return to the Land of Promise.* Second, God promised a *restoration of the land.* Third, God promised a *realization of each of His previous promises* to Adam, Noah, Abraham, Moses, and David. Fourth, God promised a *renewed heart.* Fifth, God promised the *removal of sin.* Sixth, God promised a *reunion of Israel and Judah under one ruler,* Jesus Christ. Finally, God promised the *realization of redemption* (this was the final covenant, and, as such, it secured redemption).

Following the exile, God raised up the prophets Haggai, Zechariah, and Malachi to continue speaking to His people. Though there is a small fulfillment of a restored temple, people, and land under the leadership of Zerubbabel, Ezra, and Nehemiah, the promises of God could not be completely fulfilled until Jesus Christ came.

Christ, the Center of the Covenant Story
The Gospels record for us the amazing truth of the incarnation. Jesus came to earth as a baby who was conceived of the Holy Spirit and lived a life of perfect obedience, died for the sins of God's people, was raised as the firstfruits of the resurrection, and ascended to the Father. Acts 2 records that the Holy Spirit was sent on the day of Pentecost to renew the church and establish it by His power.

The new age was inaugurated through Christ and His church, but it awaits its consummation until Christ returns to bring the old age to a complete end with the final judgment and usher in the new heaven and the new earth. In the meantime, the church is to fulfill the Great Commission, a topic we will address further in chapter 9.

It is only in Christ that the Covenant King and the covenant servants meet. Christ is the Lord of the covenant and the Servant of the covenant. He has come as Lord to extend grace and mercy to God's rebellious servants, and He has come as the Servant of the covenant to perfectly fulfill what God's people could never fulfill, thus bringing blessing to all those who place their faith in Him. Since all the promises of God are Yes and Amen in Christ (2 Cor. 1:20), the covenantal context of Scripture necessitates that we connect each passage to Christ.

The story of Jesus begins in the Old Testament in the opening chapters of Genesis, with the account of creation. As the apostle John so eloquently says, "In the beginning was the Word, and the Word was with God, and the Word was God. He was in the beginning with God. All things were made through Him, and without Him nothing was made that was made. In Him was life, and the life was the light of men. And the light shines in the darkness, and the darkness did not comprehend it" (John 1:1–5). Paul echoes this truth in Colossians 1:15–17: "He is the image of the invisible God, the firstborn over all creation. For by Him all things were created that are in heaven and that are on earth, visible and invisible, whether thrones or dominions or principalities or powers. All things were created through Him and for Him. And He is before all things, and in Him all things consist."

Like John, Matthew doesn't begin his gospel account with the birth of Jesus but rather with the genealogy of Jesus Christ, reaching back through the pages of the Old Testament to Abraham. Luke goes back even further in his gospel, tracing the story of Jesus all the way to Adam, the son of God (Luke 3:38). Paul also traces the story of Jesus back to Adam when he says, "And so it is written, 'The first man Adam became a living being.' The last Adam became a life-giving spirit" (1 Cor. 15:45). Even before the fall, the first man Adam pointed forward to the greater and final Adam, Jesus Christ. Luke closes his gospel with Jesus's own version of His story, so we should pay close attention as we read this account in Luke 24.

Two disciples were trying to put the story of Jesus together as they walked home from Jerusalem. They had just witnessed the events that had happened at the end of Jesus's life. And now they had seven long miles to try and figure things out as they journeyed home from Jerusalem to Emmaus. But they couldn't understand. In fact, they were deeply distressed. Their hope had been deflated. They thought that Jesus was the one who had come to redeem Israel, but instead He was crucified and buried. Indeed, they had learned that the tomb was empty, and Jesus was nowhere to be seen. Note carefully what Jesus says to them, "'O foolish ones, and slow of heart to believe in all that the prophets have spoken! Ought not the Christ to have suffered these things and to enter into His glory?' And beginning at Moses and all the Prophets, He expounded to them in all the Scriptures the things concerning Himself" (Luke 24:25–27).

Wouldn't you have liked to walk those seven miles with the three of them? It was the greatest walk those disciples would have in their entire lives as the Master Teacher told His own story, beginning in Genesis and moving all the way through the Prophets. It was not the privilege of these two disciples only to hear Jesus tell His story; it was the privilege of the twelve disciples also. Luke tells us later in the same chapter that Jesus opened their minds to understand the Scriptures, everything written about Him in the Law of Moses and the Prophets and the Psalms. These things had to be fulfilled, and Jesus was telling them that He was the fulfillment (Luke 24:44–45).

He is the second Adam who did not sin but was obedient to death on the cross. He is the Seed of the woman who crushed the serpent's head (Gen. 3:15). He is the final Noah who saved His people through the cross. He is the final Abraham in whom all the families of the earth are blessed. He is the final Isaac who was sacrificed for our sin. He is the final Passover Lamb (Ex. 12:13). He is the final sacrifice whose blood atoned for our sins (Lev. 16:14–16). He is the final and perfect priest who is greater than Aaron. He is the true Israel who was tested and tried in the wilderness and passed (Matt. 4:1–11). He is the one lifted up to deliver sinners from death (Num. 21:9). He is the prophet greater than Moses (Deut. 18:15–22). He is the one who gives grace to covenant breakers (Deut. 27:1–26). He is the ark of the covenant and the blood on the mercy seat (Heb.

9:11–14). He is the true bread of life and the light of the world on the golden lampstand (John 6:48, 51; 8:12). He is the Commander of the army of the Lord (Josh. 5:14). He is the final judge who never fell into sin but delivered His people by taking their judgment for them (2 Cor. 5:21). He is the final kinsman-redeemer greater than Boaz (Ruth 3:12–13). He is the final psalmist who leads His people in praise to God (Heb. 2:12). He is the final Davidic king who reigns in perfect justice and righteousness (John 18:37). He is the final Solomon who is not only full of wisdom but is wisdom Himself (1 Cor. 1:30). He is the final prophet who suffered for His people and did so without opening His mouth in retaliation (Isaiah 53). And He is the Great Shepherd of the sheep (Ezek. 34:11–24).

Peter is proof that Jesus opened their minds to understand that day, for in Acts 2 we read Peter's sermon, in which he cites David's words in Psalm 16:8–11 and finishes by citing David's words in Psalm 110:1, with these words in between:

> Men and brethren, let me speak freely to you of the patriarch David, that he is both dead and buried, and his tomb is with us to this day. Therefore, being a prophet, and knowing that God had sworn with an oath to him that of the fruit of his body, according to the flesh, He would raise up the Christ to sit on his throne, he, foreseeing this, spoke concerning the resurrection of the Christ, that His soul was not left in Hades, nor did His flesh see corruption. This Jesus God has

raised up, of which we are all witnesses. Therefore being exalted to the right hand of God, and
having received from the Father the promise of
the Holy Spirit, He poured out this which you
now see and hear. (Acts 2:29–33)

We cannot tell the story of Jesus any way that we
please. We must learn from Jesus Himself and tell the
story beginning with Genesis through Deuteronomy,
moving through the Prophets and the Psalms, and then
the New Testament Gospels and Letters, closing with
Revelation, where the end of the story is told: "I saw a
new heaven and a new earth, for the first heaven and the
first earth had passed away" (Rev. 21:1). Of course, the
end of the story isn't really the end, for we will spend an
eternity worshiping "Him who is and who was and who
is to come…Jesus Christ, the faithful witness, the first-
born from the dead, and the ruler over the kings of the
earth," the One who loves us and has freed us from our
sins by His blood and made us a kingdom and priests to
His God and Father (Rev. 1:4–6).

Maybe you've had the privilege of being raised in a
church that has taught you covenant theology all your
life, or maybe you are learning about covenant theology for the first time. Regardless, I hope this chapter
has whet your appetite to study the Bible with a compre-
hensive understanding of the covenant story, including
a covenantal framework by which to interpret Scripture

that emphasizes a redemptive-historical, Christ-centered approach.[4]

Thinking It Through

- Jot down your present sin, suffering, and service in light of what you have learned about covenant theology in this chapter.

    Sin—

    Suffering—

    Service—

- What did you learn about the covenantal context of Scripture in this chapter that you didn't know before?

- What have you learned in this chapter about interpreting Scripture in a Christ-centered way?

---

4. See my Bible studies on Hebrews; Judges and Ruth; 1 Peter, 2 Peter, and Jude; and Revelation for further help on doing this. They are listed in the bibliography.

Chapter 4

All of Grace

One of my favorite periods of history is the Reformation of the sixteenth century. One year I spent the month of October, in anticipation of Reformation Day on October 31, reading *Reformation Heroes* with my oldest children. It was wonderful to read the stories of Martin Luther, John Knox, John Calvin, and many other Reformers, and it was convicting as I was reminded how hard Protestant men and women fought for the truth of justification by faith alone through grace alone.

I readily confess justification is by faith alone, but I have to admit that when I take a close look at my heart I see something inside that wants to be a part of earning my salvation. This has been clearest to me during times of failure. In each instance, I was tempted to either make up what I had cost the other person or punish myself for not performing well. For example, if I failed to play according to my coach's expectations in high school, I punished myself by not eating. If I failed to make a decent dinner for my family, I offered to make a new one. When I made an editorial mistake in one of my Bible study books, I offered to pay my publisher if it cost them money to correct the error (thankfully, it didn't). Over time the Lord graciously revealed to me that I had a difficult time accepting grace when it was extended, wanting to work to pay off my mistake instead.

I'm sure you can relate. As fallen creatures, we want to have something to do with our own salvation. We believe that if we keep a list of rules perfectly or are a good enough person, we can contribute to our salvation and somehow pay God back for the gift He has given us in Christ. But Scripture is clear that salvation is of the Lord (Jonah 2:9). Even trying to pay God back reveals a complete misunderstanding of the gift He has given us in Christ Jesus. In this chapter, then, I want to help us understand the justification, adoption, and sanctification believers have received through the covenant of grace, but first let's review what we've already learned in previous chapters. In chapter 1 we learned that God has chosen to enter into a covenant relationship with His people. We also saw that it is important to learn the overarching story of Scripture in order to form a covenantal worldview. In chapter 2 we learned that God has given us a covenant book, the Word of God, so that we can know Him and His will. And in the last chapter we learned about key covenants in redemptive history, the covenant story, and how Christ is the center of that story. Now we are going to take a closer look at how Christ's death, which He explains in covenantal terms, "This cup is the new covenant in My blood, which is shed for you" (Luke 22:20), has accomplished our justification, adoption, and sanctification.

The Golden Chain of Salvation

A favorite verse of many Christians is Romans 8:28: "And we know that all things work together for good to those who love God, to those who are the called according to His purpose." I rarely hear them quote Romans 8:29–30 with it: "For whom He foreknew, He also predestined to be conformed to the image of His Son, that He might be the firstborn among many brethren. Moreover whom He predestined, these He also called; whom He called, these He also justified; and whom He justified, these He also glorified." Theologians have referred to these verses as the golden chain of salvation, and rightly so. They are golden in their truth and contain precious promises that should deeply comfort our hearts. Let's take a brief but closer look at what each of these doctrines means—foreknowledge, predestination, calling, justification, and glorification.

First, God's foreknowledge is the beautiful truth that before the foundation of the world, God knew us and divinely initiated a relationship with us.[1] We see this truth clearly in Ephesians 1:3–4: "Blessed be the God and Father of our Lord Jesus Christ, who has blessed us with every spiritual blessing in the heavenly places in Christ, just as He chose us in Him before the foundation of the world." This is an incredible truth to ponder. What woman do you know who doesn't want to be known? Who doesn't want to be chosen? Who doesn't want to have a relationship initiated with her? Our covenant

---

1. Douglas Moo, *The Epistle to the Romans,* The International Commentary on the New Testament (Grand Rapids: Eerdmans, 1996), 533.

God has chosen us to be His! He had a relationship with you in mind before the creation of the world.

Second, God predestined us, which means He had a purpose behind His electing grace,[2] and this purpose is spelled out in Romans 8:29: "to be conformed to the image of His Son." Or as Ephesians 1:4 says, "that we should be holy and without blame before Him in love." Why? Romans 8:29 says so "that He might be the first-born among many brothers." Genesis tells us that God made Adam and Eve in His own image, but sin has marred the image of God within humankind. Part of the covenant of redemption (which we studied in chapter 3) among the three persons of the Trinity is to restore the image of God in believers. This is the purpose of predestination, which helps explain many of the events of our lives. What happens to us from day to day is not a set of random events but a purposeful set of events chosen by our heavenly Father in order to make us more like Jesus.

Third, God called those whom He knew before the foundation of the world as His own in real space-and-time history, and His call was effectual. It was a call that could not be resisted by the one chosen. All those whom God has chosen will be His because His grace is irresistible. In question 31, the Westminster Shorter Catechism defines effectual calling as "the work of God's Spirit, whereby, convincing us of our sin and misery, enlightening our minds in the knowledge of Christ, and renewing our wills, he doth persuade and enable us to embrace Jesus Christ, freely offered to us in the gospel." This is

2. Moo, *Romans*, 534.

incredibly encouraging when we are praying for the salvation of our loved ones. I pray daily that the Lord will save my children. I know I can't do it because salvation is of the Lord. But it is a precious truth to me that my children, if and when they are called, cannot resist God's grace.

Fourth, God justifies His children. By the time we reach these verses in Romans 8, Paul has already written at great length about justification in his letter to the Romans. God has declared us not guilty anymore in Christ Jesus. It is by grace alone through faith alone in Christ alone that we are saved. In question 33 the Westminster Shorter Catechism defines justification as "an act of God's free grace, wherein he pardoneth all our sins, and accepteth us as righteous in his sight, only for the righteousness of Christ imputed to us and received by faith alone."

Notice that justification is an act of God's free grace. We don't contribute to our justification; salvation is of the Lord. He pardons His people's sins because Christ bore the wrath for them on the cross of Calvary. We should have died, not Christ, but He took our sin and shame upon Himself and died a cursed death on our behalf. Furthermore, God the Father accepts His people as righteous because they are clothed in Christ's righteousness. In answer 60, the Heidelberg Catechism says it beautifully: We are righteous before God "only by true faith in Jesus Christ. Although my conscience accuses me that I have grievously sinned against all God's commandments, have never kept any of them, and am still inclined to all evil, yet God, without any merit of my own, out of

mere grace, imputes to me the satisfaction, righteousness, and holiness of Christ. He grants these to me as if I
had never had nor committed any sin, and as if I myself
had accomplished all the obedience which Christ has
rendered for me, if only I accept this gift with a believing
heart." So Christ not only died for us but also lived a life
of perfect obedience for us. This brings great assurance
of faith. If we didn't do anything to gain our justification,
then we can't do anything to lose our justification.

When I am tempted to think that I am unworthy to
stand before my Father, whether it's in the wake of sin
and shame or because of an innocent editorial error, it
is a deep comfort to remember that God the Father still
says, "This is my beloved daughter with whom I am well
pleased" because I am clothed in the righteousness and
perfection of His Son. This doesn't take away from my
need for repentance for my sin before Him, but it frees
me from despair, drying my repentant tears and moving
me back into fellowship with Him, knowing that I am
accepted in Christ.

Finally, God glorifies His children. He never leaves
the process incomplete. God preserves all those whom
He calls until the day of glorification. In Romans 8:30,
glorification is stated as if it has already occurred, and
in God's eyes, it has. His decree is eternal. His word will
not return void. His grace will never fail. All those who
are foreknown, predestined, called, and justified will
certainly be glorified. According to the Westminster
Shorter Catechism, question 38, "At the resurrection,
believers, being raised up in glory, shall be openly
acknowledged and acquitted in the day of judgment,

and made perfectly blessed in the full enjoying of God to all eternity."

Adoption

Adoption, like justification, is also an act of God's free grace. Out of His love for us, God the Father has adopted us into His family, and He is not ashamed to call us His children (1 John 3:1–2). We have received the Spirit of adoption, and it is the Spirit by whom we have the incredible privilege to cry, "Abba! Father!" It is the Spirit who testifies to our spirit that we are God's children—indeed, even heirs of God and fellow heirs with Christ (Rom. 8:14–17). As God's children we not only receive His blessings but also His loving discipline in order to conform us more and more to Christlikeness (see WLC, A. 74).

My husband is adopted, so I have had the privilege of seeing a tangible expression of adoption play out before my eyes. There is nothing that my in-laws have ever said or done that would lead you to believe my husband isn't their biological child. They have loved him, cared for him, and claimed him as their son with pride and joy in their voices. So too our heavenly Father loves us, cares for us, and claims us as His own. One of my favorite words in prayer is "Father." To come before my Father, who has adopted me as His child, and lay my suffering, sin, shame, and service at His feet is an incredible blessing. It comforts me in suffering, convicts me in sin, and strengthens me in service. To know that my Father will never forsake me is a precious truth indeed.

Sanctification

We have seen then that both justification and adoption are acts of God's free grace. Now we come to the doctrine of sanctification, which is the *work* of God's free grace. This distinction is important to understand, so let's take some time to unpack it. Although we cannot separate justification and sanctification, we need to recognize they differ at three points. First, in justification God imputes (ascribes) the righteousness of Christ to us. This is a once-for-all act that can never be undone. We stand before our Father robed in the righteousness of Christ. But in sanctification, the Holy Spirit infuses (puts within the believer) grace and enables believers to exercise it, so that they can say no to sin and yes to righteousness.

Second, in justification God freely pardons our sins because of Christ's perfect life of obedience and His atoning death. But in sanctification, our sin is subdued. We are no longer under the dominion of sin, but remnants of sin are still in every part of us, and our flesh is still at war against the spirit. That means we must, by God's grace, fight the good fight and strive for holiness. Finally, in justification God frees all of us equally and perfectly from His wrath so that we can never fall under God's condemnation. But in sanctification the degree of holiness is not the same in all of us, nor is it perfect in this life because we have not yet been completely freed from the remnants of sin that still taint every part of us and won't be completely freed until Christ comes again to glorify us (see WLC, A. 77, 78).

With these three distinctions in mind, let us recall that sanctification is by God's grace. How can it be otherwise? Left to ourselves we don't want to share, or tell the truth, or give glory to another. Therefore, we cannot boast in our sanctification any more than we can boast in our redemption. Paul tells us that Jesus "became for us wisdom from God—and righteousness and sanctification and redemption—that, as it is written [in Jeremiah 9:23–24], 'He who glories, let him glory in the LORD'" (1 Cor. 1:30–31). So we are already sanctified in Christ, yet sanctification is also progressive. The Lord is progressively renewing our whole selves after His image. His Spirit enables us more and more to say no to sin and yes to righteousness. We don't just "let go and let God." But neither do we chug up the mountain of sanctification saying, "I think I can, I think I can, I think I can," and when we achieve some kind of victory over sin say, "I thought I could, I thought I could, I thought I could." Instead, we strive for holiness, we fight the good fight, and we fix our eyes on Christ, the author and perfecter of our salvation, while we constantly cry out in dependence on our Father, "Help me! Make me strong! I can't do this without Your strength." Our sanctification will not be complete until we reach glory. Until the day we die, you and I will still sin. But it's important to remember that this truth didn't keep Paul from laboring in prayer and proclamation to exhort his brothers and sisters to holiness. Likewise, the author of Hebrews tells us to strive for the "holiness, without which no one will see the Lord" (Heb. 12:14).

Sanctification by grace does not lead to licentiousness on the one hand or legalism on the other. Instead, it leads to a heart motivated by the loving grace of God to walk in the good works He has prepared beforehand for us to do by His enabling grace. The design of the gospel is salvation from something to something. We have been saved from sin in order to be a sanctified people for God's own glory.

Better Benefits

The world around us talks a lot about benefits. What's in it for me? is a common question. The doctrines we looked at in the golden chain of salvation, as well as adoption and sanctification, have better benefits than this world can ever offer because they are enacted on "better promises" (Heb. 8:6). The Westminster Shorter Catechism, answer 36, reminds us what the benefits of justification, adoption, and sanctification are for the believer: "assurance of God's love, peace of conscience, joy in the Holy Ghost, increase of grace, and perseverance therein to the end." Isn't that beautiful? We can know for certain that God loves us. When our own flesh, the world, or the devil accuses us of being too sinful, too full of shame to be His, we can have peace of conscience that we are His beloved daughters. When the storms of life threaten our happiness, the Holy Spirit gives us true joy. During difficult times of suffering or under temptation to sin, He gives more grace. And the Spirit will empower us to persevere in such assurance, peace, joy, and grace regardless of our circumstances.

Perhaps you can relate to my temptation in the midst of failure either to repay the cost of my mistake or punish myself for not performing well. Maybe you too have realized that you have a difficult time accepting grace when it is extended, wanting to work to pay off your mistake instead. Perhaps you have thought that if you keep a list of rules perfectly or are a good enough person, you can contribute to your salvation and somehow pay God back for the gift He has given you in Christ. I hope this chapter has reminded you that Christ's covenantal death perfectly and eternally secured our justification, adoption, and sanctification so that we can have assurance of our Father's love for us, peace of conscience when the devil accuses us of our sin, joy in the Holy Spirit when suffering threatens to undo us, increase of grace in the midst of living life in a fallen world, and perseverance in the faith as we look with hope for the city that is to come.

Thinking It Through

- Jot down your present sin, suffering, and service in light of what you have learned in this chapter about the doctrines of the golden chain of salvation.

Sin—

Suffering—

Service—

- How would it change your attitude and actions if you recognized the following:

  You stand before God robed in the righteousness of Christ?

  You are part of the family of God?

  You are responsible to strive for holiness by the Spirit's enablement?

- How does the Westminster Shorter Catechism, answer 36, encourage you?

Chapter 5

But God

It was my sophomore year of high school, and I was sitting around with my cross-country teammates listening to the older girls compare fat grams in bagel brands. If you have ever looked at bagel labels, you know there isn't any difference worth noting unless you are obsessed with your weight. Little did I know how influential that conversation (and many more like it) would become in my life. Add to that the billboards, magazines, and other media that boasted model-thin women all around me, and I bought into the lie that I have to be model-thin in order to be beautiful. In other words, I believed that my worth was based on my outward appearance.

At the same time I was running cross-country, I was also playing basketball. Unlike my teammates on my cross-country team, my teammates on my basketball team were not having conversations about fat grams in bagel brands. They could eat a Big Mac in no time at all and not think twice about it. And my coach certainly thought I could use a few Big Macs myself in order to put on some weight for my position as forward or center. There was another conversation going on though

within basketball that was just as influential and just as
damaging as the one on my cross-country team. It really
wasn't a conversation at all. It was a coach with a tem-
per who could fire off a cuss word, stomp his feet, clap
his hands, and throw water, attempting to motivate us to
play better and harder. Failing to live up to his expectations led me to believe another lie: my worth is based
on my outward performance. Failure to perform well
led me to inflict punishment on myself, which matched
perfectly with the motivation behind the other lie—if I
didn't live up to my coach's expectations, then I didn't
deserve to eat.

By the time I was in college, my addiction to thinness
and fitness was raging. *But God* intervened. I still remember sitting in my Hebrew class during my final exam with
tears streaming down my face as I translated the verses in
Jonah from Hebrew to English:

> The waters surrounded me, even to my soul;
> The deep closed around me;
> Weeds were wrapped around my head.
> I went down to the moorings of the mountains;
> The earth with its bars closed behind me forever;
> *Yet You have brought up my life from the pit,*
> *O LORD, my God.* (2:5–6, italics mine)

Our lives are filled with "but God" moments, times
when God reaches down and saves us out of pits. But
there is one pit that is greater than all others, and that
is the pit of our utter unbelief when we are dead in our
sin. There is also one rescue that is greater than all others, and that is the rescue from sin and shame to light

and life in Christ. This is the greatest "but God" moment of our lives.

Let's take just a moment though to review what we've already learned in this book. In chapter 1 we learned that God has chosen to enter into a covenant relationship with His people. We also saw that it is important to learn the overarching story of Scripture in order to form a covenantal worldview. In chapter 2 we learned that God has given us a covenant book, the Word of God, so that we can know Him and His will. In chapter 3 we learned about key covenants in redemptive history, the covenant story, and how Christ is the center of that story. And in the last chapter we learned about the justification, adoption, and sanctification believers have received through the covenant of grace. In this chapter I want to help us understand more clearly that all humankind are covenant breakers, that the Covenant King has chosen out of His love and grace to save some of us, and that our salvation is secured by Christ's fulfillment of the covenant of grace.

By Grace You Have Been Saved
In his letter to the Ephesians, Paul takes great pains to present the gospel to the saints so that they will know the love of Christ and live in light of it. He begins his letter by telling them who they are—saints who have inherited numerous spiritual blessings in Christ. Then he tells them what they once were in order to magnify the amazing grace of God in Christ Jesus:

> And you He made alive, who were dead in

trespasses and sins...and were by nature children of wrath, just as the others.

   But God, who is rich in mercy, because of His
great love with which He loved us...made us alive
together with Christ (by grace you have been
saved), and raised us up together, and made
us sit together in the heavenly places in Christ
Jesus, that in the ages to come He might show
the exceeding riches of His grace in His kindness
toward us in Christ Jesus.... For we are His work-
manship, created in Christ Jesus for good works,
which God prepared beforehand that we should
walk in them. (Eph. 2:1, 3–7, 10, italics mine)

Don't rush past the "but God" in this passage. Highlight
it in your Bible. Keep it in your mind. Don't ever forget
you once were dead in sin, but now, only by the grace of
God, you are alive in Christ.

The Doctrines of Grace
Ephesians 2:1–10 unfolds for us five truths that are
extremely important to grasp. First, Paul says we are cor-
rupt in every part of our being (Eph. 2:1–3; WCF 9.3–5).
The fall impacted every part of us—mind, body, and soul.
To the extent that one person is more evil than another
person is only a difference of degree, not of kind. All of
us have fallen short of the glory of God. Not one of us
is good. This truth should humble us. We are not better than the person beside us. Fallen humanity is in the
same boat. We are dead in our sin, completely unable to
respond positively to God without His intervention. This

truth also reminds us that we are dependent on the Lord in evangelism to awaken the souls of the spiritually dead and, as such, should be an encouragement for us to fervently pray the Lord will open the blind eyes, unstop the deaf ears, and soften the hard heart of the one to whom we proclaim the kingdom of God and teach about our Lord Jesus Christ.

Second, we are chosen by God's grace to be His people (Eph. 2:4–5; WCF 3.3–5). There is nothing I have done to earn God's favor or to make Him want to choose me as His child. I am just as dead as everybody else. But God sovereignly chooses those He will call His family for His own glory and purposes and because of His great love. This truth, like the previous one, should greatly humble us. We must understand that there is nothing we have done to earn our salvation. Therefore, there is nothing we can do to lose our salvation. This is immensely freeing for those of us who are performance driven. God didn't choose us because we performed well. It's not as if we made the team because we were able to play good defense and offense. He is not the coach who yells at us when our performance is poor and praises us when our performance is perfect. Instead, He is the gracious Father who has chosen us in Christ to be His children and in love both blesses us and disciplines us just as a father blesses and disciplines his children.

Third, we are certain that our salvation is of the Lord. God's redemption of His people is not a possibility but a certainty (Eph. 2:6–7; WCF 3.1). When God breathed new life into us and saved us by His grace alone, He purposed to save us completely and finally.

There is great assurance of our salvation in knowing that our redemption is not just possible but certain. All those for whom Christ died will be saved. His death was meant to accomplish the salvation of God's people, and it won't fall short of the exact number God has sovereignly chosen to be His own. This should give us peace not only with regard to our own salvation but also with the salvation of our loved ones. In other words, we can never be kicked off the team, and neither can our loved ones. As an athlete, I knew that there was certain behavior that would not only get me benched for a game but would put me off the team. I lived under that knowledge, knowing I could lose my spot if I failed to obey the rules. That is not how it is for the child of God. When David had an affair with Bathsheba, he sinned greatly (2 Sam. 11:1–12:25; Psalm 51), but he didn't lose his place in the kingdom of God, and neither will you or I. Must we confess and repent when we sin? Absolutely. But we confess and repent before a Father who has secured our salvation through the blood of His Son, Jesus, and stands ready to receive us with forgiving arms.

Fourth, we are called out of darkness and death into light and life (Eph. 5:8; WCF 10.1). Since we are dead in our sin, the Spirit has to call us out of death into new life in Christ. This call is certain and effective because God has purposed our salvation. We cannot resist God's grace calling us from darkness into light. This truth should motivate us to proclaim the gospel to people from every nation. The Lord uses His people to proclaim the gospel so that more and more people might come to know Him through the Spirit's effective call. It should also motivate us to pray and proclaim the gospel to our covenant children and the covenant children in our churches. The Spirit is at work and often uses our prayers and proclamation to bring others to saving faith.

Fifth, we can be confident that He who began a good work in us will complete it at the day of Jesus Christ (Eph. 2:10; Phil. 1:6; WCF 17–18). The Lord preserves us as we persevere in the faith. We cannot lose our salvation since salvation, from start to finish, is of the Lord. This should greatly encourage us when we see our loved ones battling the flesh, the world, and the devil. When the Lord saves someone, He finishes the job. It's not up to us to complete His work, whether that is in ourselves or in someone else. As we walk alongside our sisters struggling with sin, growing weary in suffering, or exhausted in service, we don't have to wring our hands as if it's up to us to complete what God has begun. We can entrust them to the One who preserves His people and encourage them to look to Him.[1]

Perhaps you can relate to my love for the phrase "but God" and my story that goes along with it. I hope you

---

1. These five points have also been called the five points of Reformed theology or the five points of Calvinism. The acronym TULIP, which stands for total depravity, unconditional election, limited atonement, irresistible grace, and perseverance of the saints, has often been used to help people remember these points, though there is some argument that better terms could be found to articulate the points more accurately (e.g., radical depravity instead of total depravity and particular redemption instead of limited atonement).

will find the time to recall your own "but God" story and write it down. Such stories force us to stop and see how rich the doctrines of grace have been in our individual lives and help us encourage our sisters with the encouragement we have received. And they help us understand more clearly that all humankind are covenant breakers, that the Covenant King has chosen out of His love and grace to save some of us, and that our salvation is secured by Christ's fulfillment of the covenant of grace.

Thinking It Through

- Jot down your present sin, suffering, and service in light of what you have learned about the doctrines of grace in this chapter.

  Sin—

  Suffering—

  Service—

- How do the doctrines of grace help you better appreciate and understand the love of God?

- Write out your own "but God" story.

Part 2

Appreciating the Beauty
of Covenant Community

Chapter 6

A Different Kind of Community

Over the years I have been blessed with many spiritual mothers, women in the faith who were willing to spend time with me, speaking truth into my life. Jackie helped me navigate my high school and early college years, lending a listening ear as we walked many miles together at a park every week. Joye mentored me through seminary, helping me evaluate my heart and not just fill my head. Gerry helped me navigate my first full-time women's ministry position, modeling for me a love for teaching God's Word. Linda put my first Bible study on the publisher's radar, and the publisher accepted it. Jane was willing to challenge some of my thoughts to make me a better author. Kathy baked muffins for me when I had a newborn and spent a day at my home re-covering my dining room chairs while talking about life.

But one woman in particular stands out in my mind. I will never forget the first year the Lord placed me in a leadership position for women's ministry. I was eighteen years old and was leading women who were older than I was and in very different seasons of life. Many of them needed counseling for troubled marriages and in other areas of life I had never experienced. But Paulette chose to place me in leadership and exhorted me with the same words Paul used to exhort Timothy: "Let no one despise your youth, but be an example to the believers in word, in conduct, in love, in spirit, in faith, in purity" (1 Tim. 4:12). That made a deep impression on me at a young age. I don't know where I would be today if it weren't for Paulette and others who have encouraged me. Each one has reminded me of the necessity and the beauty of covenant community.

Two Sides of the Same Coin

In part 1 of this book, my goal was to help you appreciate the beauty of covenant theology. Now, in part 2, my goal is to help you appreciate the beauty of covenant community. But I want to clarify an important point. Appreciating the beauty of covenant theology and appreciating the beauty of covenant community are two sides of the same coin. Appreciating the beauty of covenant community flows from appreciating the beauty of covenant theology.

Titus 2 illustrates this point. Titus is one of Paul's last letters. It is known as a pastoral epistle because Paul is writing to a young pastor, Titus, with a specific purpose in mind for the church. He is writing "according to the faith of God's elect and the acknowledgment of the truth" (Titus 1:1). In the first part of his letter, Paul gives Titus qualifications for elders. Then, in the second part, he instructs Titus on teaching what accords with sound doctrine. But he does not just assign this job to Titus. Instead, he assigns it to older men in the faith to teach the younger men and older women in the faith to teach the younger women (Titus 2:3–5).

We must not forget that the foundation of older women teaching younger women is sound doctrine. If we do not have sound doctrine, then we cannot teach younger women in the faith what is good; we cannot train younger women to love their husbands and children, to be self-controlled, to be pure, to be working at home, and to be submissive to their husbands in a way that will not discredit the Word of God. It is important to note that the difference is not whether we will teach them; the difference is how we will teach them.

We also must not forget that Paul's instruction for right living is grounded in what God has already done for us in Christ: "For the grace of God that brings salvation has appeared…Jesus Christ, who gave Himself for us, that He might redeem us from every lawless deed and purify for Himself *His own special people*, zealous for good works" (Titus 2:11–14, italics mine). Notice Paul's emphasis on the corporate—Christ gave Himself for *us*, to redeem *us*, to purify *a people for Himself*. What kind of community is this that Jesus Christ, the Lord of all creation, would give Himself to them?

The Church
If we want to study the church, we must begin in the book of Genesis, not in the book of Acts. The Seed of the woman is Christ, but it also includes the church since Christ is the head of the church. From the one man Adam comes the one family of Abraham, from whom comes the one nation of Israel, from whom comes the

remnant of the New Testament church. Thus, Pentecost was the renewal of the people of God, not the beginning.

Peter gives us a beautiful definition and description of the church in the language of the Old Testament: "But you are a chosen generation, a royal priesthood, a holy nation, His own special people, that you may proclaim the praises of Him who called you out of darkness into His marvelous light; who once were not a people but are now the people of God, who had not obtained mercy but now have obtained mercy" (1 Peter 2:9–10). These verses remind us that we are in a covenant relationship with others. When our heavenly Father adopted us, we became part of the family of God. I am not an only child, and neither are you. We have a multitude of brothers and sisters from every tribe, tongue, and nation.

It is the Lord who said it was not good for man to be alone at creation (Gen. 2:18). Community is God's idea. Indeed, the triune God lives in community as three persons: Father, Son, and Holy Spirit. But with the fall came sin and suffering, which led to shame and secrecy, which resulted in individualism and isolationism. It is not nakedness that differentiates Adam and Eve before the fall and after the fall but shame and works righteousness. We see this in Genesis 2:25: "And they were both naked, the man and his wife, and were not ashamed." We also see it in Genesis 3:7: "Then the eyes of both of them were opened, and they knew that they were naked; and they sewed fig leaves together and made themselves coverings."

Satan subtly seduced Eve into self-reliance. And Adam and Eve were both shamed into "fig-tree righteousness," trying to cover up what had already been exposed by God, an impossible thing to do. Thankfully, we don't have to read very far before learning of God's grace. He clothes Adam and Eve's shame with grace—the grace of animal skins, which foreshadowed the Lamb of God to come, Jesus Christ, who would take the curse of our sin upon Himself, freeing us from self-reliance to be God-reliant and freeing us from isolation to interdependence in the community of grace.

Individualism and isolationism continued to plague humankind throughout the history of redemption. After initially responding "I don't know," Cain answered the Lord's question, "Where is Abel your brother?" with another question many people are still asking today: "Am I my brother's keeper?" (Gen. 4:9). Scripture answers this question by picking up the story line of Genesis 4 in 1 John 3:11, the context of which is John's exhortation to the church to love one another. We are our brothers' and sisters' keepers. We are to know where they are and what they are doing not to condemn them, but to encourage them and exhort them in the ways of the Lord.

True Community
One of the greatest privileges I have when counseling women is to walk alongside them in the dark places of life. It takes great courage for my sister to make the phone call or send the email to cry for help. But when she does, she often recognizes the beauty of covenant community.

Asking for help is extremely difficult to do though, even in the church. Most of us continue in our secret shame, not wanting others to know of our sin and

suffering. We think we will ruin our reputation if we
expose our struggles, so we continue sewing fig leaves
together to make loincloths to cover our shame. The
problem is, our solution never satisfies; instead, it leaves
us anemic in the area of community, robbing us of God's
design for humankind.

Consider the Tower of Babel in Genesis 11, humanity's futile attempt to create community: one language,
one people, one location, one common goal—to make
a name for themselves. But the people failed to acknowledge the one Lord who is over all, and they were judged
because of it. The Lord dispersed them over the face of
the whole earth. There can be no true community apart
from God. The day of Pentecost was the reversal of the
Tower of Babel. The Lord brought clarity where there
had once been confusion. He brought unity where there
had once been division. He brought His power where
there had once been humanity's attempt at power.

True community is found only in Christ, the one who
brought us near by His blood, giving us His peace, making us one new man in place of the two, reconciling us
both to God in one body through the cross (Eph. 2:13–
16). Therefore, we are to be eager "to keep the unity of
the Spirit in the bond of peace. There is one body and
one Spirit, just as [we] were called in one hope of [our]
calling; one Lord, one faith, one baptism; one God and
Father of all, who is above all, and through all, and in
you all" (Eph. 4:3–6).

Life Is Not about Me

Scripture's teaching stands in stark contrast to society's teaching, which has made it especially easy for us to think individually about our faith. Our culture places a strong emphasis on the individual, sending us the message in a thousand different ways that life is all about us. Tragically, this mind-set has crept into the church and is now largely accepted. There are many people today who don't think going to church is all that important because "it's about me and my relationship with God" and not with the covenant community. But this ignores the covenantal context of Scripture that we talked about in chapter 3.

We see the concept of community in the covenant of redemption, in the covenant of works, and in the covenant of grace. In the covenant of redemption, all three persons of the Godhead are working out our redemption. The Father chose us, the Son has redeemed us, and the Spirit seals us, guaranteeing the possession of our inheritance (Ephesians 1). In the covenant of works, *all* died through Adam's trespass (Rom. 5:12–14). And in the covenant of grace, in Christ *all* God's people are made alive (Rom. 5:15–20).

There are other ways in which the theme of community recurs in Scripture. Community is not just God's idea; it is a reflection of His character. From the beginning it was not good for man to be alone, so God made a helper for him (Gen. 2:18). Also, God chose Israel to be the people of God, a kingdom of priests and a holy nation (Ex. 19:4–6; 1 Peter 2:5–9), the congregation

that comes together to worship and enter into covenant
(Ex. 19:7–8; Heb. 12:22–24).

In the New Testament we see the body of Christ,
with Christ as the head and the various parts represent-
ing members (Eph. 4:11–16); the vine and the branches
(John 15); the living stones being built into a spiritual
temple (1 Peter 2:4–5); and the importance of the family that serves as a model for the church (Col. 3:18–24).
The importance of family is seen in that God's promise is not just for individuals but also for families (Jer.
32:39). Peter's words on the day of Pentecost illustrate
this: "For the promise is to you and to your children, and
to all who are afar off, as many as the Lord our God will
call" (Acts 2:39).

We are bound by covenant to God and to one
another, while at the same time we retain our individual-
ity in the midst of community. We need one another if
we are going to grow up in every way into Christ. Otherwise, we will remain as children, tossed around by the
waves and winds of deceitful doctrine.

Individuals in Community
In rightly emphasizing the importance of covenant community, we must not forget that we all stand before the
Lord as individuals as well. No one else's faith can save
us. In the end, our name must be in the Lamb's Book
of Life, which is the ultimate reason we believe in Jesus
Christ as our Lord and Savior. So, dear reader, do you
love Jesus? Do you know Him? Do you worship Him? Do
you nurture others in the faith, pointing them to Him?
Do you witness to the world about Him?

Passing the Faith to the Next Generation

Covenant theology leads to community life that is governed by the God of the covenant. God's covenant love, His loyal lovingkindness, is to govern all our relationships with our neighbors. Covenant community flows from covenant theology. Over and over in Scripture we learn that we are to pass the faith from one generation to another, not just in our individual families but in our covenant communities as well. Psalm 145:4–5 says,

> One generation shall praise Your works to another,
> And shall declare Your mighty acts.
> I will meditate on the glorious splendor of Your majesty,
> And on Your wondrous works.

If we do not understand the concept of covenant, we will be anemic in the area of community. But if we have a firm grasp on the truth that the God of the covenant builds a covenant community and that the covenant promises are for us and for our children, then we will realize that we are not just going to another event, taking another class, or filling another slot in the nursery. We will understand that we are fostering fellowship with one another, growing in the grace and knowledge of Jesus Christ together, and keeping our promise to help train up our covenant children in the faith. The primary way we pass the faith to the next generation is through the means of grace. The means of grace are a beautiful expression of the covenant, and they include the Word of God, prayer, and the sacraments (baptism and the Lord's Supper). Let's take a closer look at each of these and why they are vitally important for our spiritual growth within the context of covenant community.

The Means of Grace

The Word of God

We should be women of the Word, seeking truth and direction from Scripture, God's covenant word to us, and submitting ourselves to its authority. The covenant Lord speaks to us through His Word as we submissively listen. It is significant that we are not the only person in the pew on Sunday morning. We sit under the preaching of God's Word in the midst of the community of God's people. The Lord uses this means not only to initially convince us of the truth but also to continue growing us together in holiness and comfort.

Another wonderful way to be in the Word together as sisters is through women's Bible studies. Over the years I have learned so much from my sisters as we gather together weekly to dig deeply into Scripture. Studying Scripture in the context of covenant community sharpens us. Not only do we learn from our sisters' answers to exegetical and theological questions but we learn from our sisters' shared struggles with suffering, sin, and service.

As we prepare to sit under the preaching of the Word at a gospel-centered church on Sundays, we should pray for our pastor as he prepares to deliver the sermons, asking the Lord to give him sound doctrine, diligence, wisdom, faithfulness, a love for God and the people in the congregation, and sincerity of heart that longs for God's name to be exalted and the people edified (see

WLC, A. 159). Then we should show up and support
him. He is, after all, the mouthpiece of God. It is not as
if we can listen with a yawn and take it or leave it. We are
called to attend upon the Word diligently, prepare our
hearts to receive it, pray as we're listening, examine what
we hear with the Word of God, receive the truth with
readiness of mind, meditate on what we hear, hide it in
our hearts, and bring forth the fruit of it in our lives (see
WLC, A. 160). Imagine what church would be like if we
all did that!

Prayer

We should be women of prayer, pouring out our hearts
in communion with our heavenly Father. The covenant
Lord communes with us in prayer as we cry, "Abba!
Father!" Corporate prayer is a beautiful picture of the
community of God coming together in agreement, asking the Lord to shine forth His Word and continue His
great work. We need prayer not just to draw closer to the
triune God but to draw closer to one another as well.
As we pray for one another, the Lord deepens our love,
which is rooted in His grace.

In his letter to the Ephesians and in the context of
spiritual warfare, Paul exhorts his readers to be people
of prayer—not just prayer, but persevering prayer (Eph.
6:18). We must pray at all times. Prayer places us in a
posture of humility. It gives us an opportunity to acknowledge our absolute dependence on someone outside
ourselves—our heavenly Father—to grant us our neces-
sities as well as our desires. In prayer, we should seek
the help we need to glorify God and enjoy Him forever.

We should pray for the salvation of others. We should pray that we would know, obey, and submit to God's will. We should pray that the Lord would grant us our daily needs. We should pray we would forgive, as He forgave us. We should pray that the Lord would keep us from the temptation to sin and support and deliver us when we do sin. In prayer, we should acknowledge that the kingdom, the power, and the glory belong to the Lord forever (see the Lord's Prayer in Matthew 6:9–13).

We must also pray in the Spirit. Romans 8:26–28 teaches us that the Spirit helps us to pray. Since we don't know what to pray for, the Spirit intercedes for us according to God's will. For those who love God and are called according to His purpose, all the things that happen in our lives work together for our good. Our good does not mean our happiness, although there will be many times when what the Lord does brings us happiness. Our good means our sanctification, and although this will not always bring us happiness, it should bring us joy as we acknowledge and rejoice in what the Lord is doing in our lives to bring us to maturity in the faith.

We must pray with alertness too. Remember that this exhortation is found in the context of Paul exhorting us to put on the whole armor of God in order to stand firm against the schemes of the devil. Praying with alertness acknowledges that we are in a battle and must be on guard against the devil at all times. To help me remember this I use answer 127 from the Heidelberg Catechism as a daily prayer: "By ourselves we are too weak to hold our own even for a moment. And our sworn enemies—the devil, the world, and our own flesh—never stop attacking us.

And so, Lord, uphold us and make us strong with the strength of your Holy Spirit, so that we may not go down to defeat in this spiritual struggle, but may firmly resist our enemies until we finally win the complete victory."

Finally, we must pray for the saints. This keeps us from becoming self-absorbed in our prayer life and acknowledges that we are part of a covenant community—the body of Christ, which He is bringing to maturity and complete sanctification. But prayer for the saints is also something we are commanded to do in Scripture. Prayer matters. It is one of the means the Lord uses to accomplish His purposes in our lives and in the lives of others. Prayer is hard work, and it is a labor of love for our brothers and sisters in Christ, our neighbors, and our family and friends as we take them before our heavenly Father. Prayer is a privilege, as it gives us the opportunity to be part of others' lives by way of intercession. I can honestly say there are few things I would rather be doing than praying. When I bring my brothers and sisters before our Father in heaven, interceding for them in their suffering, their sin and shame, or their service, I not only grow in love for them but I also long for the Lord to use them to glorify His great name.

The Sacraments

Not only should we be women of the Word and women of prayer but we should also be women who eagerly participate in the sacraments. The covenant Lord nourishes our souls as we receive the sacraments. Baptism and the Lord's Supper are family events. We are baptized in front of the covenant community, and we partake of the Lord's Supper together as the family of God.

Baptism is the outward sign of our entrance into God's kingdom. We are baptized into the name of the triune God. Far from coming to a program, we come to a person. Far from coming to a club, we come to Christ. Far from a place we pay dues, Christ has paid our dues for us. Far from entering the doors of an organization, we are surrounded by the church of Christ, a living organism organized by the God of order. Baptism is our admission into the visible church, the community of believers, the family of God. We are one in Christ Jesus.

Baptism marks not only our new name but also our new heart. The Lord sprinkles clean water on us, giving us a new heart and a new spirit (Ezek. 36:25–26). Baptism also marks our union with Christ. Paul tells us that all of us who have been baptized into Christ Jesus have been baptized into His death so that we might walk in newness of life. We have been united with Him in both death and resurrection. We have died with Christ, and now we live with Him (Romans 6). Baptism is also the outward sign of the inward seal of the Holy Spirit for our salvation. As those who have been given the Holy Spirit, we are to respond in covenant commitment to walk in newness of life together.

When infants are baptized in some covenant communities, church members are asked to raise their hands or stand up and respond, "I do" and commit to helping the parents raise these little ones in the fear of the Lord. This is a beautiful reminder of the covenant community's responsibility to pass the faith from one generation to another. When we're at church, as tempting as it is to compliment a little girl on how beautiful she looks in her dress and bows, perhaps we should spend more time asking her what beautiful truths she learned about the gospel in Sunday school. You just might be amazed at the response you get!

The Lord's Supper is for our spiritual nourishment and growth in grace. It is a covenant meal. It is not only a bond and pledge of our communion with Christ but also with one another as members of His body. Unlike baptism, which is a one-time event, the Lord's Supper is a continual covenant meal reminding us of our communion with Christ and with the people He purchased by His own blood. As surely as we taste the bread and the wine, so Christ gave Himself for us and lives in union with us. Because there is one Christ and one loaf, there is one body, one church. Our union with Christ means that we are also united to one another, and this makes a different kind of community indeed!

I hope that you, like me, have been blessed with many spiritual mothers in the covenant community. And I hope that you fervently desire to be a spiritual mother to younger women the Lord has placed in your life. Perhaps there is a young woman in your church today who needs your help through her years of high school or college. Maybe a young woman needs your encouragement to step into a leadership role. Perhaps a seminary student needs your help to evaluate her heart. Maybe a young mom needs your help in her home, discussing life issues with her through a covenantal worldview. Paul reminds us that our mentoring mission in the covenant community is grounded in hope: "For the grace of God that brings salvation has appeared to all men, teaching us that, denying ungodliness and worldly lusts, we should live soberly, righteously, and godly in the present age, looking for the blessed hope and glorious appearing of our great God and Savior Jesus Christ, who gave Himself for us, that He might redeem us from every lawless deed and purify for Himself His own special people, zealous for good works" (Titus 2:11–14).

Thinking It Through

- Jot down your present sin, suffering, and service in light of what you have learned about the covenant community in this chapter.

Sin—

Suffering—

Service—

- How have spiritual mothers impacted your life? How are you being a spiritual mother to a younger woman?

- Based on what you have learned in this chapter, how would you define the church? How has what you have read helped you appreciate it?

- How do you prepare to eagerly participate in listening to the Word of God each week?

- Describe your prayer life. What changes would you like to implement?

- How does what you learned about the sacraments in this chapter encourage you?

Chapter 7

From Life Taker to Life Giver

Girls today are growing up in a culture that minimizes and even rejects the idea and importance of biblical womanhood. The covenant community must be a place where they hear a different answer. We must help them understand the difference between male and female as it relates to every aspect of life, including the home, the workplace, and the church. We must teach our girls, as well as the women in our churches who were never taught or who have forgotten, that women are life-giving helpers who are to bring the gospel to bear on every circumstance of life and are to serve the covenant community with their spiritual gifts.

Defining Womanhood
The place to start defining womanhood is a bit like Maria's song in the *Sound of Music*:

> Let's start at the very beginning
> A very good place to start
> When you read you begin with A-B-C
> When you sing you begin with Do-Re-Mi.

We might make up a new line: "When you define womanhood, you begin with chapters 1, 2, 3 [of Genesis, that is!]."

The triune God made man in His image (Gen. 1:26–27). Adam and Eve, as image-bearers, were to be living representations of the Creator, the one who gives life. As image-bearers, they were equal. As male and female, they were distinct. So too the Father, the Son, and the Holy Spirit are the same in substance and equal in power and glory, yet at the same time they are three distinct persons.

It was the Creator God who breathed life into Adam so that the man became a living being (Gen. 2:7). But he would not be the only living creature. Community is the Creator's idea. The Lord God said it was not good for the man to be alone, so He made a helper fit for the man. He made the first woman from Adam's rib and brought her to Adam (Gen. 2:18, 21–22). After Adam and his wife fell into sin, he "called his wife's name Eve, because she was the mother of all living" (Gen. 3:20). The phrase "mother of all living" can also be translated from the Hebrew as "life giver." When we think of the context of this verse—it follows God's curse on the serpent and the difficult consequences He gave to Adam and Eve for their disobedience—it is amazing to think of Adam naming Eve the mother of all living. Shouldn't she be named Death Giver or Mother of All Dying? Apart from God's grace, that is exactly what she would have been. Because of the fall, Eve did not have the ability to be a life-giving helper. Instead, she was a life taker, taking life out of others. Eve needed a Redeemer to enable her

to be a life-giving helper again. And indeed, God promised one in Genesis 3:15:

> And I will put enmity
> Between you and the woman,
> And between your seed and her Seed;
> He shall bruise your head,
> And you shall bruise His heel.

This promise, which Adam heard with ears of faith, is the
reason he could call his wife Eve, life giver. What a beautiful testimony of God's graciousness to Adam and Eve.
Each time Adam called her name, he would be reminded
of God's promise to raise up a greater Life Giver one day.
As we saw in chapter 3, this promise of a Life Giver is
worked out throughout the history of redemption. As we
move from Genesis toward the New Testament, we see
God preserving the godly line until Jesus Christ, the final
and perfect Life Giver, is born in Bethlehem.

As those who are in Christ, we have been brought
from death to life. It is not just Eve, then, but all women
who are created to be life-giving helpers. This design
cannot be fulfilled apart from God's grace. Apart from
Christ, we take life out of others, hurting them and hin-
dering them from bearing God's image. But in Christ,
we are able to give life to others, helping them to bear
God's image. As His image-bearers, we are to speak life-
giving words (Prov. 15:31; Phil. 2:16), display life-giving
actions, and give life-giving gifts. As we do so, we reflect
God's light and life to a dead and dark world in desperate need of the good news of the gospel.

Since we are in the process of sanctification until Christ returns, we don't do this perfectly. Our lives reveal that we have taken life out of certain situations and given life to other ones. It is far easier to take life than give life. For example, when I've put in a long day with the children and am anxiously waiting my husband's arrival, I'm hard-pressed to say, "No problem, honey" when he calls and says he is going to be late. There is a war going on in my heart at that moment. Often, I utter a brief prayer: "Father, help me to breathe life into this situation by responding to my husband with grace." Other times I fail to respond with grace in situations and must repent of my sin, rest in my Redeemer's forgiveness, and return to being a life-giving helper again.

Biblical Portraits of Womanhood

Proverbs 31:10–31 is a beautiful picture of a redeemed woman, created to be an image-bearer, who is a life-giving helper to all those around her. Her foundation is the fear of the Lord (v. 30). She knows she is a creature made by the Creator and a kingdom disciple with the kingdom task to make disciples of all generations by passing down the faith. She knows she was created to be a life-giving helper, and, in light of such knowledge, she blesses her husband, children, and neighbors. She knows her life is in the Promised One and that she is to be an aroma of that life to others. She knows and shows God's compassion to the poor and needy. She is known and praised in the community because of the life-bearing fruit of her hands—the good works that God prepared beforehand for her to do. She speaks life-giving words of wisdom and teaches kindness.

In the New Testament, we reach the climax of the history of redemption—the life, death, resurrection, and ascension of Jesus Christ. Jesus is the true helper and life giver. He came so that we might have life, and have it to the full (John 10:10). He is the way, the truth, and the life (John 14:6). Paul tells us that it is the Spirit who gives life (2 Cor. 3:6) and is our helper (John 14:26) and that God's Word is the word of life (Phil. 2:16). He also tells us that it is God who gives life to everything (1 Tim. 6:13). This is the lens through which we must read Proverbs 31. None of us can be a Proverbs 31 woman unless we are united to Christ, and even then, on this side of glory, we will not do so perfectly. Think of Sarah, for example. She is commended in the New Testament as a holy woman whose hope was in God and who adorned herself with submissiveness to Abraham (see 1 Peter 3:6). Yet in the Old Testament we learn that Sarah was impatient to wait for God's promise of a son, taking matters into her own hands and giving her husband her servant with whom to have a child. The result was disastrous. Sarah looked upon her servant Hagar with great contempt, dealing harshly with her, and had to face the truth that Hagar and Abraham's son, Ishmael, would be against everybody and everybody would be against him (see Genesis 16).

In the New Testament, we continue to see women who are life-giving helpers. Mary, Jesus's mother, trusted God's word and gave birth to Jesus, raising Him in a home that feared the Lord (Luke 1:26–38). Elizabeth,

John the Baptist's mother, breathed life into Mary's circumstances by recognizing she was chosen of the Lord to carry Jesus (Luke 1:39–45). The woman at the well became a life giver when she testified to her townspeople about Christ (John 4:27–30). The women who left the empty tomb were life givers when they proclaimed the resurrection (Luke 24:1–12). Martha and Mary were life givers as they served Jesus (Luke 10:38–42). Priscilla was a life giver to her husband in ministry (Acts 18:26). Phoebe was a life giver as a servant-leader in the church (Rom. 16:1). Tabitha was a life giver as a woman of prayer and good works (Acts 9:36). Lydia was a life giver as a woman of prayer, faith, and hospitality (Acts 16:14–15). And Lois and Eunice (Timothy's grandmother and mother) were life givers who modeled their sincere faith for Timothy (2 Tim. 1:5). These women should serve as examples for us to be life-giving helpers to those around us. But how will we do this?

Recognizing the Power of the Gospel
Second Peter 1:2–4 says,

> Grace and peace be multiplied to you in the knowledge of God and of Jesus our Lord, as His divine power has given to us all things that pertain to life and godliness, through the knowledge of Him who called us by glory and virtue, by which have been given to us exceedingly great and precious promises, that through these you may be partakers of the divine nature, having escaped the corruption that is in the world through lust.

Life-giving helpers must be gospel-centered women. We must live out the truth that God's power has granted to us all things that pertain to life and godliness. *All things.* The next time someone tells you there is no hope for change, remember that is a message devoid of the gospel of grace. There is hope for change precisely because there is Someone changing us. The same power that raised Jesus from the dead is at work in you and me to conform us more and more to the image of Christ.

We must also live out the truth that we have become partakers of the divine nature. It is an amazing thought that we are in union with Christ. We have died with Christ and are now free from the dominion of sin. We have also been raised with Christ so that we might walk in newness of life.

Being a gospel-centered woman also means that we live out the truth that we have escaped from the corruption that is in the world because of sinful desire. We are no longer servants of Satan but are servants of the Covenant King. We have been transferred from the kingdom of darkness to the kingdom of light.

Finally, as the verses that follow 2 Peter 1:3–4 teach us, we make every effort to supplement our faith with Christlike character—virtue, knowledge, self-control, perseverance, godliness, brotherly kindness, and love (see 2 Peter 1:5–7).[1] Faith is active. Our motivation is what God has done for us (His indicatives). Our track is

---

1. To study these qualities further, see my Bible study on 1 Peter, 2 Peter, and Jude.

what we are to do in response to what He has done (His imperatives). We run by God's grace, but we still run.

Forgetting the Gospel

If we are to be life-giving helpers who are gospel-centered, why do our lives often look so different? Why do we sometimes speak words of death, yell in anger, utter words seasoned with judgment, and have hearts cold as stone? Peter tells us in 2 Peter 1:8–12:

> For if these things are yours and abound, you will be neither barren nor unfruitful in the knowledge of our Lord Jesus Christ. For he who lacks these things is shortsighted, even to blindness, and has forgotten that he was cleansed from his old sins....
>
> Be even more diligent to make your call and election sure, for if you do these things you will never stumble; for so an entrance will be supplied to you abundantly into the everlasting kingdom of our Lord and Savior Jesus Christ.
>
> For this reason I will not be negligent to remind you always of these things, though you know and are established in the present truth.

Peter teaches us in these verses that if the qualities he mentioned in the previous verses (such as virtue, knowledge, and self-control) are not ours and are not increasing, we have become ineffective and unfruitful in the knowledge of the Lord Jesus Christ. This is because faith without works is dead (James 2:14–17). The person who has been saved by faith alone is also the person who works out his or her own salvation with fear and trembling, recognizing it is God who works in them both to will and to do for His good pleasure (see Phil. 2:12–13).

There is another lesson we learn from these verses. If we lack these qualities, we have become so nearsighted that we are blind, having forgotten that we were cleansed from our former sins. Failing to grow in godliness reveals we have failed to grasp the gospel. Oftentimes this leads to us believing and teaching a moralistic ("Be a good person, and you will be saved"), legalistic ("Do this, and you will live"), or therapeutic message ("I'm good, you're good, God is good, everything is okay") to those around us. In contrast, gospel-centered women believe and teach that we were saved from slavery to sin in order to be God's special people, and as His special people, we are to reflect His holiness. God's deliverance should motivate us to grow in godliness.

Finally, Peter teaches us in these verses that if we do not continually remind each other of these qualities, even though we are established in the truth, we easily forget and become women who know the gospel intellectually but not practically. In other words, Peter is not content to move on from the gospel, as if there are more important things to teach and preach. Instead, Peter recognizes that we need to be reminded of the gospel every day of our lives, even though we know we are to grow in holiness as part of our salvation and even though we are well established in the truth.

Perhaps you have a daughter who is growing up in our culture that rejects and minimizes the idea and importance of biblical womanhood. If so, I hope and pray this chapter has encouraged you to give her a different answer. Or maybe you never learned the biblical definition of womanhood, and you are hearing it for the first time. I want to encourage you that it's never too late to begin being a life-giving helper. The covenant community must be a place where we proclaim the truth that women are life-giving helpers who are to bring the gospel to bear on every circumstance of life.

Thinking It Through

- Jot down your present sin, suffering, and service in light of what you have learned about biblical womanhood in this chapter.

  Sin—

  Suffering—

  Service—

- What have you learned in this chapter about the truth that you were designed to be a life-giving helper? In what present circumstance do you need to be a life giver instead of a life taker?

- How have you recognized, or failed to recognize, the power of the gospel in your

  Marriage—

  Parenting—

  Relationship with a friend or coworker—

  Ministry—

Chapter 8

Speaking the Truth in Love

Late one night after the children were in bed, my husband and I were having a disagreement. He had had a long, tiring day at work, so he sat in my study chair and slumped down. I was tired too, but I was also upset, and there wasn't another chair in the room, so I remained at my standing desk, where my Bible lay open from my morning study. The more I spoke, the less my husband spoke, so I took advantage of having a quiet audience and picked up my Bible that lay next to me to speak truth to my husband. You can well imagine how that night would have gone over if the Holy Spirit hadn't convicted my heart in the middle of it and opened my eyes to see how I would look to any bystander, standing up with my Bible in hand while my husband slumped in my study chair. I literally burst out laughing at the ridiculousness of the matter (and my manner!), and thankfully neither of us went to bed angry at each other. There is a big difference between speaking truth and speaking the truth in love.

Growing Up Together

In the letter to the Ephesians, in the context of unity in the body of Christ and of Christ equipping God's people with spiritual gifts, Paul contrasts mature manhood with immature childhood. In contrast to children carried about by false doctrine, the body of Christ, *while speaking the truth in love*, is to grow up in every way into Christ. Christ, "from whom the whole body, joined and knit together by what every joint supplies," as each part does its own work, makes the body grow, so that it builds itself up in love (Eph. 4:16). This is an amazing picture of corporate growth. The Lord uses our brothers and sisters to sanctify us and uses us to sanctify our brothers and sisters. The key is speaking the truth in love.

Community life is not always beautiful. Sometimes it is ugly, messy, and complicated. It is hard not to feel naked and ashamed when others know our deepest suffering and sin. Yet the Lord promises to redeem our broken communities and to build them into beautiful ones precisely *because* they are in desperate need of His grace. Jesus did not come to those who were healthy, but to the sick. He did not come to call the righteous, but sinners. He breaks into our broken communities and begins a good work that He promises to complete. This is good news! As we share our lives with others and as others share their lives with us, we have the hope that He who began a good work in us, and in them, is still working and will not stop until the work is done.

Speaking in Truth and Love

Sisters who have grievously sinned, been grievously sinned against, or both will come to us. We must speak the truth to them in love. We must always remember, as we walk with them through their crisis, to point them to the Good Shepherd, Jesus Christ, the one who redeems their stories for their good and His glory and who is coming again to make all things new.

We must begin by giving them a covenantal worldview, helping them see their small story as part of the larger story of redemption. We must remember that all Scripture is profitable for teaching, reproof, correction, and training in righteousness (2 Tim. 3:16). Yet we must also choose wisely what text or book of the Bible might best help them. Above all, we must connect the text we are studying to both their problem and to the gospel; Christ alone is where their hope must rest. The Heidelberg Catechism's answer to question 1 says it beautifully, "What is your only comfort in life and in death?"

> That I am not my own, but belong with body and soul, both in life and in death, to my faithful Saviour Jesus Christ. He has fully paid for all my sins with His precious blood, and has set me free from all the power of the devil. He also preserves me in such a way that without the will of my heavenly Father not a hair can fall from my head; indeed, all things must work together for my salvation. Therefore, by His Holy Spirit He also assures me of eternal life and makes me heartily willing and ready from now on to live for Him.

The Bible teaches that God loves us and has called us to be saints (Rom. 1:7). Philippians 1:6 says that God has begun a good work in His people. So we should always encourage our sisters by telling them where we see God's grace in their life and where we see them running the race of grace well. The Bible also teaches that we will suffer for Christ's name's sake (Phil. 1:29). So we should acknowledge and empathize with our sisters' suffering and point them toward Bible passages that will comfort them. One of my favorite go-to passages is Isaiah 43:1–3:

> Fear not, for I have redeemed you;
> I have called you by your name;
> You are Mine.
> When you pass through the waters,
>   I will be with you;
> And through the rivers,
>   they shall not overflow you.
> When you walk through the fire,
>   you shall not be burned,
> Nor shall the flame scorch you.
> For I am the LORD your God,
> The Holy One of Israel, your Savior.

The answer to question 26 of the Heidelberg Catechism offers comfort as well:

> That the eternal Father of our Lord Jesus Christ, who out of nothing created heaven and earth and all that is in them, and who still upholds and governs them by His eternal counsel and providence, is, for the sake of Christ His Son, my God

and my Father. In Him I trust so completely as to have no doubt that He will provide me with all things necessary for body and soul, *and will also turn to my good whatever adversity He sends me in this life of sorrow. He is able to do so as almighty God, and willing also as a faithful Father.* (italics mine)

Finally, the Bible teaches that we will continue to sin on this side of glory (Gal. 5:17). So we must be willing to confront our sisters' sin, speaking the truth in love, while recognizing that we are a sinner too.

Most importantly, we must cover our sister in prayer. We should pray with her when we are together and when we are apart. We are powerless to change her, but prayer is powerful, and the Holy Spirit works through our prayers and our counsel to redeem the most grievous of situations. Our hope is not in the person changing. Our hope is in the Lord who can change the person. Paul calls us not only to speak the truth in love but also to walk in love, light, and wisdom (Eph. 5:1–21).

Walking in Love
In Ephesians 4 Paul tells us that we are to walk in a manner worthy of the calling to which we have been called. We have been called to the one hope that belongs to our call—one Lord, one faith, one baptism, one God and Father of all, who is over all, through all, and in all (Eph. 4:1, 4–6). Paul also tells us that we must no longer walk as unbelievers do, in the futility of their dark minds and hard hearts, because that is not the way of Christ.

Paul goes on in Ephesians 5 to tell us that, as God's children, we are to walk in love because Christ loved us and gave Himself up for us. Because Christ gave Himself up for us, we are to give up the immorality and impurity that used to characterize our lives, and we are to put on the purity of Christ (5:1–5). This is countercultural, but it is necessary. When my daughter asked me, "All the other moms let their daughters wear pants like that. Why can't I?" I had the opportunity to train her in modesty. But purity is far more than outward apparel. I have had plenty of conversations with my children, beginning at a young age, about how important sexual purity is. It is imperative we train our children in the purity of Christ. We are to strive for pure thoughts, words, motives, and hearts, knowing it is the Lord who gives us the power for pure living.

Walking in Light

We are also to walk as children of light because we are light in the Lord (Eph. 5:8–9). Our lives should bear the fruit of light—goodness, righteousness, and truth. Such fruit flows from eyes focused on God's Word. Psalm 119:130 says, "The entrance of Your words gives light."

My husband works for a lighting company, so lights are a big deal at our house. I'm always amazed at how he can spot dust on the crystal chandeliers when I can't see even a speck. He wants them to be spotless because the light shines so much brighter when the dust is removed. It gives me a good illustration of my own walk with Christ. So often I am walking around like a dusty chandelier, filled with sin that hinders my light from shining as it should. Christ calls us to let our light shine before all men so they may see our good deeds and glorify our Father in heaven (Matt. 5:16).

Walking in Wisdom

Finally, we must walk in wisdom because Christ became to us wisdom from God (1 Cor. 1:30). This means we must make wise use of our time (Eph. 5:16). Each of us could name great time wasters in our life that steal our focus from where it needs to be. Scripture tells us to lay aside every weight, and sin that clings so closely to us, and to run the race that is set before us with endurance, while we fix our eyes on Jesus, the founder and perfecter of our faith (Heb. 12:1–2). If you are not sure what your time wasters are, take a day to record how much time you spend on different activities (eating, cooking, social media, emails, and driving). You'll be shocked! And it just might help you start eliminating unnecessary activities and streamlining necessary ones.

I had a seminary professor who was asked how he accomplished all that he did. He graciously replied, "I don't do what you do." Living in community is costly. We will often have to say no to things we might really want to do in order to do what we should do. For example, I may have to say no to things you say yes to in order to prepare to speak at a women's retreat or teach a Bible study or write a book. All of us are responsible to steward our time well for God's glory.

Walking in wisdom also means we must understand what the will of the Lord is (Eph. 5:17). I used to agonize over decisions. What college should I go to? What seminary should I attend? Which man should I marry? I remember wanting a blinking light in the sky or a post-card in the mail. If the Lord would only tell me or if I could only find it, I would do it! But God's will is not something you have to find. God has a plan for our lives to be sure, but He is orchestrating it, not us. He rules over our lives, providentially bringing events to pass to accomplish His will for us.

It is true that Scripture gives us some definite answers to the question, What is God's will? These include 1 Thessalonians 5:18: "In everything give thanks; for this is the will of God in Christ Jesus for you." We also have 1 Peter 2:15: "For this is the will of God, that by doing good you may put to silence the ignorance of foolish men." But understanding what the will of the Lord is for our lives comes mostly by studying all Scripture and applying its wisdom to decisions. James 1:5 is a great encouragement as we seek to do so: "If any of you lacks wisdom, let him ask of God, who gives to all liberally and without reproach, and it will be given to him."

Walking in wisdom also means that we must be filled with the Spirit (Eph. 5:18–21). This means we do not grieve the Holy Spirit of God, by whom we were sealed for the day of redemption, and it results in a different way of life. We will sing and make melody to the Lord with our hearts. The Spirit enables us to sing a song of grace. When we are so overwhelmed with what Christ has done for us, we will not be able to stop singing! We will give thanks always and for everything to God the Father in the name of our Lord Jesus Christ. A great prescription for grumbling and unbelief is gratitude. We have much to be thankful for, and specific thanks for specific blessings should be on our lips often. We will be women of kindness, tenderheartedness, and forgiveness. Even when someone isn't kind to us, we will be kind to them. When someone is going through a tough time, our hearts will be tender toward them. When someone sins against us, we will readily forgive them, remembering how much Christ has forgiven us. We will submit to one another out of reverence for Christ. Living in community means living submissively. We not only look out for our own interests but for those of others (Phil. 2:4). And we will address one another in psalms and hymns and spiritual songs. How do we do this?

Paul says, "Let the word of Christ dwell in you richly in all wisdom, teaching and admonishing one another in psalms and hymns and spiritual songs, singing with grace in your hearts to the Lord" (Col. 3:16). Make it a practice to be in the Psalms every day. Begin or end the day with the hymnal. Over time, write out a hymn or spiritual song of your own. Then be in the Psalms with others, sing hymns with others, and share spiritual songs with others.

Hearts and Hands of Compassion

Not only does Paul call us to speak the truth in love and walk in love, light, and wisdom but he also calls us to have hearts and hands of compassion that reach out to the covenant community and to the world (Col. 3:12). God's covenant love is His merciful, compassionate, loyal lovingkindness:

> The LORD is gracious and full of compassion,
> Slow to anger and great in mercy.
> The LORD is good to all,
> And His tender mercies are over all His works.
>   (Ps. 145:8–9)

His compassion is seen throughout Scripture and in the covenantal structure. That God would condescend to make a covenant with His creatures is the greatest act of compassion. But it doesn't end there. All throughout the history of redemption, we see Him having compassion on His people, extending grace and mercy when they deserve wrath and judgment.

Note Exodus 6:5–8, for example:

> And I have also heard the groaning of the children of Israel whom the Egyptians keep in bondage, and I have remembered My covenant. Therefore say to the children of Israel: 'I am the LORD; I will bring you out from under the burdens of the Egyptians, I will rescue you from their bondage, and I will redeem you with an outstretched arm and with great judgments. I will take you as My people, and I will be your God. Then you shall know that I am the LORD your God who brings you out from under the burdens of the Egyptians. And I will bring you into the land which I swore to give to Abraham, Isaac, and Jacob; and I will give it to you as a heritage: I am the LORD.

In Scripture the Lord specifically mentions the poor, the widow, and the orphan. He looks after the brokenhearted and the neglected. A beautiful example of this is in Exodus 22, the context of which are various laws concerning social justice. The Lord says to His people, "If you ever take your neighbor's garment as a pledge, you shall return it to him before the sun goes down. For that is his only covering, it is his garment for his skin. What will he sleep in? And it will be that when he cries to Me, I will hear, for I am gracious" (Ex. 22:26–27). What a beautiful picture of God's compassionate love! And we, as His covenant people, are to be the same.

Paul writes to the saints and faithful brothers in Christ at Colossae: "Therefore, as the elect of God, holy and beloved, put on tender mercies, kindness, humility, meekness, longsuffering" (Col. 3:12). Notice that he grounds the imperative in the indicative. We show compassion because Christ first showed compassion to us.

How do we show compassion to others? We serve those in need. We join with other women in small groups to do service projects. We pray and ask God to show us who in our life needs to be shown compassion and then expectantly watch to see the opportunities God gives. We pray for our persecuted brothers and sisters regularly. We ask our deacons of any needs among the women of the church and then combine our time and resources to tend to those. We come alongside our pastors and elders and help counsel women in crisis. We take meals to those in need. We drive women to and from Bible study, stores, or doctors if they are unable to do so. Most importantly, we model compassion toward others. Pray that you will have a heart filled with compassion, words seasoned with grace, thoughts marinated in love, hands extended in hospitality, and feet that walk the extra mile with someone in need.

Serving with Spiritual Gifts

At the beginning of this chapter, I mentioned that Paul was teaching about speaking the truth in love and about Christ equipping God's people with spiritual gifts in the context of unity in the body of Christ. I also mentioned that we should make wise use of our time, saying no to things in order to do what God has given us to do for His glory. So I want to close this chapter by briefly looking at our responsibility to serve the covenant community with our spiritual gifts. Christ is the head of the church, and each believer has been given grace according to the measure of Christ's gift. We don't choose our gifts; He does, and they are gifts of grace. They are to be used to equip the saints for the ministry and to edify the body of Christ: "Christ—from whom the whole body, joined and knit together by what every joint supplies, according to the effective working by which every part does its share, causes growth of the body for the edifying of itself in love" (Eph. 4:15–16). The Westminster Confession of Faith says that because saints are united to Christ, we are also united to one another in love and "have communion in each other's gifts and graces, and are obliged to the performance of such duties, public and private, as do conduce to their mutual good, both in the inward and outward man (26.1)."

God, in His grace, has given each of us different gifts in order to serve one another. We are not to squander our gifts, hide them, ignore them, or compete with them. We are to use them for the glory of God and the good of His people. The best way to learn our gift(s) is to serve in the church and then listen to the covenant community. What do other church members see as our gifts? Once we learn what our gifts are, we must use them for the good of the body and the glory of God (1 Peter 4:10–11).

Knowing our gifts doesn't mean we never serve in other capacities, but it does keep us focused on what our main ministry should be. If our gift is teaching, then we must study and teach well. If our gift is service, then we must serve well. If our gift is giving, then we must be cheerful givers. If our gift is leading, then we must lead zealously. If our gift is mercy, then we must show mercy cheerfully.

We are not only to listen to the covenant community concerning our gifts; we are also to help others learn theirs. And when we see our brothers and sisters serving well, we need to encourage them in their gifts, even as we faithfully exercise ours.

Can you relate to the argument I had with my husband? Have you ever spoken the truth—but not in love? There is a big difference between the two. Being a healthy part of the covenant community means we are women who speak the truth in love; walk in love, light, and wisdom; and have hearts and hands of compassion that reach out to the covenant community and to the world to serve those in need.

Thinking It Through

- Jot down your present sin, suffering, and service in light of what you have learned about speaking the truth in love in this chapter.

    Sin—

    Suffering—

    Service—

- In what circumstance do you need to speak the truth in love today?

- In what area of your life do you need to walk in love, light, and wisdom?

- How can you put on a heart of compassion and reach out to others in need this week?

- How does recognizing that God has given different people different spiritual gifts and that you are to serve Christ and His church with the one(s) He has given you affect your attitudes and actions?

- Take time to encourage a sister this week, telling her where you see her serving well.

Chapter 9

A Mandate and a Mission

In January 2009 I was enjoying time outside on our playground with my three-year-old and one-year-old. But throughout the day, I started experiencing severe GI pain with increasing intensity. By the time I was making peanut butter and jelly sandwiches for lunch, I was doubled over at the counter. I kept hoping it would resolve, but by late afternoon I had locked myself in our master bathroom, knowing something was severely wrong. By the time my husband got home from work, our two precious children had made a mess of the house, and my three-year-old greeted his daddy at the door with, "Mommy's dead." What my husband didn't know at the time was that our three-year-old's statement wasn't far from the truth. My husband, seeing the emptiness of my eyes, had to wrestle us all into the car to head to the hospital. But it wasn't long before he realized the seriousness of the situation and called an ambulance to come pick me up at the gas station where he had parked.

It was a terrible ambulance ride as I tried to twist and turn my body every way I could for relief from the pain. Finally, in the emergency room, I hazily heard the

ER doctor say I was in full-blown shock. As morphine flooded my system, my body began to relax for the first time in hours. A weekend stay in the hospital with several tests revealed the most likely scenario was that I got a kink in my colon, and, because of my good health and age, it ended up resolving on its own. I knew that day, though, ultimately it was the Lord, not my good health and age, who had kept me alive.

Two responses to my near-death experience revealed what I believed my purpose was in life. First, while I was in the hospital, I implored my dear friend and sister in Christ to raise my children the way I would. This revealed my intense desire to pass the faith to the next generation. Second, an accelerated use of my spiritual gifts after that weekend revealed my intense desire to glorify God by doing what He had created and called me to do, not knowing how long I had to serve Him and not taking my life for granted.

I have found over the years that I am not the only woman who has sought to define my purpose in life. Many of us can quote that our chief end is to glorify God and enjoy Him forever, but how? What are we to spend our days on this earth doing? The topics of this chapter, the cultural mandate and the Great Commission, answer this question.

It will be helpful if we keep the covenant story of the Bible (creation, fall, redemption, and restoration) in mind as we discuss the cultural mandate and the Great Commission. By doing so, we will see how they fit together and how they apply to us today.

The Cultural Mandate

God gave the cultural mandate to Adam and Eve on the sixth day of creation: "Then God blessed them, and God said to them, 'Be fruitful and multiply; fill the earth and subdue it; have dominion over the fish of the sea, over the birds of the air, and over every living thing that moves on the earth'" (Gen. 1:28). According to Genesis 1:28, culture is a blessing, and it is to be founded on God's Word. Human beings are to multiply and rule the world according to God's Word and for God's glory.

Humankind is made in the image of God; male and female He created them. The difference of the sexes was God's divine design for humankind. It is important to note that the cultural mandate was not given to Adam alone, but to Adam and Eve together. This is instructive; men and women need to work together to fulfill the cultural mandate. It is just as significant to note that the cultural mandate is given in the context of a blessing: "Then God blessed them" (1:28). The cultural mandate is not a burden, but a blessing.

Human beings were to multiply by bearing children. This multiplication of humankind was to be done within the context of covenant marriage. Adam and Eve needed to multiply in order to subdue the earth and have dominion over the creatures. Humankind is to rule the earth for God's glory, bringing forth from it all its potential. Following the cultural mandate we read, "Then God saw everything that He had made, and indeed it was very good" (Gen. 1:31). So culture was to come from that which was good. After God finished His work of creation, He rested. But the work of culture was not finished. It was just beginning.

The Cultural Mandate Threatened
Tragically, the beginning of culture was interrupted by the fall. And the fall had radical implications for the future of the cultural mandate. Instead of culture being grounded in God's Word, it was grounded in humanity's word. And the end was no longer God's glory, but humanity's glory.

Amazingly, the fall was not the final word. And it was not the end of creation or culture. By God's grace His purposes prevail. Within the curses that the Lord spoke to the serpent, to Eve, and to Adam in the context of the fall, the cultural mandate is revealed. Humankind would still multiply, but pain would accompany the bearing of children, and conflict would characterize the marriage relationship. Humankind would still rule and work, but it would be fraught with difficulty. The earth that people were to subdue would be full of thorns and thistles.

Graciously, God clothed Adam and Eve with garments of skins (foreshadowing the One to come, the Lamb of God who takes away the sin of the world) and sent them out of the garden to work the ground from which man came (Gen. 3:23). Immediately we see what disastrous results the fall had on the first family. Adam and Eve experienced the grief of their oldest son murdering their second son. Death threatened God's command to multiply, yet death was not the last word. The Lord would raise up a seed, Jesus Christ, to deliver humankind from death (Gen. 3:15).

A few chapters later, in Genesis 6–9, God's grace is seen in the floodwaters of judgment when He saved a remnant of humankind, Noah and his family. When Noah and his family emerged from the ark, the Lord graciously restated the cultural mandate (Gen. 9:7). Thus, the fall did not negate God's command to multiply and rule the earth, but it drastically affects humanity's obedience to it. We see this when the fallen people of the earth attempt to make culture again at the Tower of Babel (Genesis 11). Their attempt ends in God's judgment of dispersion because their end was their own glory, not His, and their foundation was their own word, not God's Word.

Throughout the story of redemption we see the cultural mandate proceed. Human beings continue to multiply and rule the world around them, but the task is fraught with difficulty and sin. Barrenness threatens the promised line. Sin threatens the Promised Land. But by God's grace, God's people (though imperfectly) carry out the cultural mandate founded on His Word with the goal of His glory while the rest of humankind attempts to make culture founded on their word and for their glory.

Jesus came to fulfill the cultural mandate but not to abolish it (the same was true for the law). He is the Seed of all seeds and the King of all kings. But that does not mean the cultural mandate has no place in the life of the church today.

The Significance of the Cultural Mandate

We touched briefly on the cultural mandate in chapter 1 in the discussion of a covenantal worldview as well as in chapter 3 when we looked at four *W*s involved in God's covenant with Adam after the fall—worship, work, woman, and the word of God, the latter of which pervades all of them. These same four *W*s can be used to sum up the significance of the cultural mandate for our lives today.

Worship Grounded in the Word of God
The cultural mandate involves keeping the Sabbath day holy. The Creator of the universe established six days of labor and one day of rest. The fourth commandment connects the Sabbath to both creation (Ex. 20:11) and redemption (Deut. 5:15). We keep the Sabbath day holy when we rest from our physical labors, rest in God's promises of eternal rest in Christ, and worship the triune God alongside our brothers and sisters in Christ.

If we don't understand why we should keep the Sabbath, we will fail to keep it. We will fail to see the importance of resting from our labors, acknowledging God as the ultimate provider. We will fail to gather together with the covenant community for worship on the Lord's Day, and we will fail to see the importance of showing covenant compassion in acts of mercy. We will fail to see the need, as covenant servants, to hear from the covenant Lord by sitting underneath the preaching of the covenant word and engaging in the sacraments.

Woman (Marriage and Family Life)
Grounded in the Word of God
The cultural mandate also involves marriage. The proper context for procreation is marriage. Not all of us are called

to marry, and not all of us are able to bear children, but for those of us who do marry and can bear children, we are our husband's helper, and we join with our husband to be fruitful and multiply, bringing forth covenant children that we train in the ways of the Lord and send out, by God's grace, as worshipers, workers, and witnesses into our Father's world. Single women and married women who cannot bear children also have the privilege and responsibility in our churches of helping to train our covenant children to love the Lord and His Word.

There is a woman at our church who has no biological children of her own, but she has impacted hundreds of our covenant children by singing God's Word to them, helping them to hide it in their hearts. It is not uncommon that I hear her voice come out of our van's CD player as the Scripture songs she recorded teach Bible truths to my children. I am deeply grateful that this woman understands and takes seriously her commitment to help parents raise their covenant children in the way of the Lord. She is training up the next generation to know and love Him.

If we don't understand the concept of covenant, we will look at our marriage as a contract that can be broken when difficulties arise rather than a covenant commitment that reflects the Lord's covenant with His people. We will look at children as a choice rather than a gift from the gracious hand of the Lord, and we will fail to see the importance of training the next generation in the ways of the Lord.

Work Grounded in the Word of God

The cultural mandate also involves labor. The Lord Himself worked (created) for six days and then rested. It takes work to subdue the earth and have dominion over the creatures. As we labor in different fields, we are to bring our greatest gifts and wisdom to bear on every situation.

If God calls us out of a career to stay at home with our children, caring for them will be no less meaningful than our career because we will understand that we are doing something of utmost importance—caring for another generation, training them up to love and serve the Lord. On the other hand, if God calls us out of the home and into a career, we will recognize that we are to contribute to the culture for the glory of God.

A Gospel Focus

As we go about fulfilling the cultural mandate, we should have a gospel focus. For example, a Christian teacher in a public school may teach the same curriculum as the non-Christian teacher in the room next door, but she will constantly be praying and thinking about how she can use opportunities with students, parents, and staff to point them to the gospel. This may be just the counsel one of your sisters needs who comes to you burned out and wondering what good she is doing in the public school.

Or take another example. A Christian man and woman who are married should have a gospel focus in their marriage and family life. Their marriage and family should reflect the grace of Jesus Christ in all aspects. A young mother who comes to you burned out from raising children may need you to remind her of the importance of her calling to make disciples of those four precious souls in her home. Rather than four walls closing in around her, she has a schoolhouse of discipleship open before her, by God's grace, with the ultimate goal of sending her children out to be worshipers, workers, and witnesses in their Father's world.

One other example comes from my own experience. I arrived at seminary at the young age of twenty-one. I was single, sixteen hours away from home, and knew no one. After looking at apartment prices in Dallas, I concluded it was more than I could afford. So I answered an ad for a seminary student to do maintenance work at a retirement center in exchange for a free room at their facility. I'm sure they expected a male student, but that year they took two females, one of them being me. It didn't take long for me to realize that scrubbing elevator tracks, changing light bulbs, and painting walls was not the only job the Lord had for me there. In fact, my entire job description changed by the time I graduated from seminary as both the management and I realized the people living there needed something far greater than new light bulbs and freshly painted walls. They needed the light of Christ to shine into their loneliness through a young girl filled with the love of Jesus. As I listened to them, laughed with them, played the piano for them, taught them from Scripture, prayed for them, and served them in a multitude of ways, I reminded them of truths they needed to hear. But it worked the other way too. Many of them reminded me of truths I needed to hear. As I sat next to men and women who had once been well-known doctors, lawyers, teachers, and other important members of society, but were now largely forgotten by the fast-paced world around them and living in one room in a four-story retirement center, I learned that living for position, promotion, prestige, power, and popularity would gain me nothing in the end. Only a life spent for Jesus, loving Him and serving Him through the ways He deems best, glorifying Him in everything we do, and worshiping Him and praying to Him will last.

The Great Commission

Before we look at the Great Commission Plan in Matthew 28, we need to remember the Great Construction Plan that precedes it in Matthew 16. In Matthew 16:18 Jesus tells us that He will build His church, and the gates of hell will not prevail against it. We must never forget that the church is a spiritual house (1 Peter 2:5), and Christ is the builder. In the Great Commission Jesus says, "All authority has been given to Me in heaven and on earth. Go therefore and make disciples of all the nations, baptizing them in the name of the Father and of the Son and of the Holy Spirit, teaching them to observe all things that I have commanded you; and lo, I am with you always, even to the end of the age" (Matt. 28:18–20).

It is significant that Jesus prefaces the Great Commission with the fact that all authority in heaven and earth has already been given to Him. He is the ruler of all, but during the time between the inaugurated kingdom and the consummated kingdom, between His first coming and second coming, He gives a word to His church: Go and sow.

For Christians living now, in the time when God's kingdom has already been inaugurated but not yet consummated, the Great Commission informs how we see the cultural mandate. The cultural mandate is still in effect, but the cultural mandate cannot be realized apart from the Great Commission. As theologian John Frame reminds us, "In the Great Commission Jesus renews God's original purpose to fill the earth with worshipers of the true God.... If the earth is to be filled with worshipers of the true God, they must first be saved from sin by the Word and Spirit of God. So, unlike the cultural mandate, the Great Commission is focused on the communication of the gospel."[1]

The Significance of the Great Commission

As with the cultural mandate, we are worshipers grounded in the Word of God. The question is not whether or not we will worship. We were born to worship, and we will worship something or someone. The question then is who we will worship and when. We are to worship God alongside one another on the Lord's Day and every other day of the week as we go about our work and our witness.

As with the cultural mandate, we are workers grounded in the Word of God. We work for the Lord for the benefit of all humankind, but we are to especially nurture our brothers and sisters in Christ. The question is not whether or not we will work. We were made to

---

1. John Frame, *The Doctrine of the Christian Life* (Phillipsburg, N.J.: P&R, 2008), 307.

work. The question is what and for whom we will work and why. We are to work for God and His glory. Christ is to be preeminent in all things.

As with the cultural mandate, we are women grounded in the Word of God who recognize that we were made to be life givers. We are to be a fragrant aroma of Christ around us, giving life to others instead of taking it from them, pointing them to our Lord and Savior Jesus Christ, the Life Giver of all life givers. But unlike the cultural mandate and because of the fall of humankind, the Great Commission adds something we don't see in the cultural mandate. We are to be women who are witnesses grounded in the Word of God, proclaiming the person and work of Jesus Christ to a lost and dying world. We are to shine the light of Christ to the world around us. We will be a witness for something. For example, we might witness for the company that employs us, telling people the company makes the best-quality beauty products or essential oils. The question is not whether or not we will witness, but who or what we will witness for and why. We are to witness for Christ.

Before we read, "Go" in the Great Commission, we need to read, "and lo, I am with you always, even to the end of the age." We do not go alone, but with the Holy Spirit, empowering us and enabling us to make disciples of all nations. The Spirit makes the disciples, opening up blind eyes and softening hard hearts to believe in the triune God, as we proclaim the gospel and teach people the commandments of the covenant word of God. Thus, evangelism and discipleship are two sides of the same coin. The church cannot do one without doing the other. Both are imperative to make kingdom disciples who understand that their chief end is to glorify God and enjoy Him forever.

We should be involved in ministries at our church, such as discipleship groups, mentoring ministries, and teaching ministries. We should seek out a younger woman or an older woman and speak into her life or ask her to speak into ours. We should be involved in missions week, learning about the importance of evangelism and discipleship in our cities, country, and around the world so that we will be better informed about how to pray for those on the field throughout the year, how to support them monetarily, and perhaps how to serve alongside them on a short-term missions trip. We should pray for our persecuted brothers and sisters, educating others about their situation, their needs, and their great desire for our prayers.

Worship, work, and witness cannot be separated from each other. Our work and our witness are grounded in our worship, which means our work and our witness reveal what we worship. For example, if we spend our days striving after the power, position, and prestige of this world, and we witness to this by how many hours we spend doing and talking about our work, we have revealed that we worship our work. Contrarily, if we spend our days seeking Christ and striving after holiness, and we witness to this by loving the Lord and our neighbor, we have revealed that we worship our Creator and Redeemer.

The cultural mandate won't be fulfilled until the Great Commission is fulfilled, and the Great Commission won't be fulfilled until Christ comes again to consummate His kingdom. But during this time between Christ's first and second coming, the "already" and the "not yet," we have great work to do.

Kingdom-Mindedness

If we are anemic in a covenantal worldview, we will be closed-minded rather than kingdom-minded, failing to remember the cultural mandate, which still applies to believers today, and minimizing the Great Commission, which works hand in hand with the cultural mandate.[2] As we pursue the cultural mandate, a covenantal worldview keeps us grounded in the truth of Genesis 1:31, "Then God saw everything that He had made, and indeed it was very good," as well as in the truth of Revelation 21:5, "Behold, I make all things new."

This means we will be kingdom-minded as we work. For example, a Christian artist paints a picture not only because art itself is good but also because that piece of art could be used to teach someone the gospel. That doesn't mean all our pictures have to be crosses instead of sunsets but that we should think and draw as a Christian, praying the picture would be used by God for His glory and for the advancement of the gospel. That might

---

2. Seeking first the kingdom of God (Matt. 6:33) is one form of the biblical goal of human life, just like the cultural mandate and the Great Commission are forms of the biblical goal, all having "to glorify God and enjoy him forever" (WSC, A.1) as the end. The kingdom of God is God's work of bringing His righteousness to earth. So in the kingdom, God and His people work to bring transformation to people and to the world. Everything we do should seek to establish God's righteousness on earth, beginning with our own lives. Frame, *Doctrine of the Christian Life*, 307.

simply mean taking some of the proceeds from the sales and putting them toward kingdom work, or it may mean having a conversation with someone who likes the piece of art and sharing our faith with them. If we understand the concept of covenant, then we will understand that we are covenant partners working for and serving our covenant Lord, doing all things for His glory (1 Cor. 10:31).

At the same time, it reminds us that we work to fulfill the cultural mandate in the midst of a fallen world and that we are to bring the message of redemption to our various spheres of influence. No one person can fulfill the cultural mandate or the Great Commission. It is truly a goal of the entire covenant community, as we all contribute together toward making disciples and impacting culture with our specific callings and gifts. Our prayer should be, "Lord, use me to bring a redemptive message to every person and every area of life we encounter, and use my brothers and sisters to do the same. Help us to glorify You and enjoy You as we endeavor to do all things well for the sake of Your holy name and the advancement of Your kingdom."

I sincerely hope you can't relate to my experience of almost losing my life, but I do hope you can relate to my desire to know my purpose in life. I hope this chapter has encouraged you to combine your gifts with others' gifts in order to fulfill the cultural mandate and the Great Commission. Let us go and proclaim the kingdom of God and our Lord and Savior Jesus Christ through our various ministries, whether at home, in the workplace, in the community, or in the church. Let our prayer be, "Father, help us to show them Your Son."

He is the image of the invisible God, the first-born over all creation. For by Him all things were created.... And He is before all things, and in Him all things consist. And He is the head of the body, the church, who is the beginning, the first-born from the dead, that in all things He may have the preeminence.

For it pleased the Father that in Him all the fullness should dwell, and by Him to reconcile all things to Himself...having made peace through the blood of His cross.

And you, who once were alienated and enemies in your mind by wicked works, yet now He has reconciled in the body of His flesh through death, to present you holy, and blameless, and above reproach in His sight—if indeed you continue in the faith, grounded and steadfast, and are not moved away from the hope of the gospel. (Col. 1:15–23)

Thinking It Through
- Jot down your present sin, suffering, and service in light of what you have learned about the cultural mandate and the Great Commission in this chapter.

Sin—

Suffering—

Service—

• How would you define your purpose in life?

• What have you learned from this chapter about
  how the cultural mandate and the Great Commission relate?

• How can you combine your gifts with others'
  gifts in order to fulfill the cultural mandate and
  the Great Commission in your home, in your
  workplace, and in your spheres of ministry?

Chapter 10

The City That Is to Come

My three-year-old son's eyes grew incredulous, and the smile that spread over his face was contagious. It was a weekday morning, and I had intentionally started a conversation with him about Jesus. He was having a hard time grasping a few theological points I was trying to bring down to his level, but when I told him that Jesus was building a place for us to come and live with Him, he completely understood and was so excited. In his little mind that loves building workshops with Dad on Saturdays at Home Depot, there was nothing better than to think that Jesus was building a place for His children. Daniel's excitement was just what I needed that day; it was a spoonful of sugar to help the medicine of suffering go down. The summer had been a long one filled with a great deal of physical pain, and I had lost my eternal perspective on more than one occasion.

One of the hardest things to do when suffering, sin and shame, or difficult service closes in around us is to keep an eternal perspective. Often I just want the physical pain to be gone right then and there, or I want to be unable to sin on this side of glory, or I want ministering to others to be easy. It is a fight to fix my eyes on Christ in the midst of difficult circumstances, and yet I can honestly say that it has been in the depths of suffering that the deepest closeness with my Father has come. It really is true that suffering is a gift from His hand.

When we find ourselves walking beside a sister in deep suffering, shame, or difficult service, one of the greatest gifts we can give her is helping her fix her eyes on Christ's return and the city to come, in which our great God will make "all things new" (Rev. 21:5). The apostle John did not say God was making all new things. Instead, God will renew this present cosmos and restore it to its right order. We can be certain of this because it's part of His covenant promise. In chapter 1 we learned that God deals with humankind by way of covenant. And the first *P* we learned to help us remember the definition of covenant was the promise of God's presence. Throughout redemptive history there has been a progression of God dwelling with His people. We learned about the garden, the tabernacle, the temple, and the climax of it all—Christ (the new temple). But God's dwelling with His people has not yet been consummately fulfilled. We must wait for Christ's return, and it should be a wait of joyous expectation, as we will learn in this chapter.

A Person

We are not just going to a place; we are going to a person. Our Lord and Savior is presently ruling in His resurrected body on the heavenly throne as King of kings and Lord of lords. He is also the Bridegroom of the church and is waiting to claim His bride. His presence in the new city will be so full of light that there will be no need for it to come from other sources. His presence in the new city ensures our place there; it is only those who are written in the Lamb's Book of Life who can enter the city.

When I got engaged I embraced loved ones and friends who congratulated me. You could not miss the joy in the conversation. We bubbled over with excitement as we talked about my wedding day to come. How I wish we clasped one another's hands more and spoke of the future marriage supper of the Lamb! How encouraging it would be to have a sister say, "Oh, Sarah, isn't it wonderful? I know you're in a great deal of pain. I know it's been a hard week. I know you are weary in service. I know you're still battling that same sin. But did you know that Jesus is coming again?"

We know Jesus is coming again. But do we really live like we know it? Too often we speak of Jesus's return with the same excitement that we speak about another mundane day of the week. Let us stir one another up to remember that our Bridegroom is coming again to claim us as His own, and let's not cease to rejoice in it!

A Possession

We are not just headed to a place and a person; we are headed to a possession. It is one thing to have someone offer you their mountain home for a week so that you can enjoy rest and refreshment with the beauty of God's creation surrounding you, but it is quite another thing for someone to buy a mountain home for you that is fully decorated and stocked with an endless supply of food and toiletries and free passes to every local attraction you could imagine. Yet our gracious God has done far more. He has not only given us a place; He has given us a multitude of spiritual blessings that come with it. We have received a possession where the dwelling place of God will be with people in all its fullness and glory.

In the city that is to come there are no tears, and there is no death, no mourning, no crying, and no pain. Think of it! The way of life that we now know, affected as it is by the fall, will be no more. No longer will addictions plague us. No longer will we watch a mother bury her child. No longer will we hear of a husband and wife who have walked away from each other after many years of marriage. No longer will we hear of terrorists or tornadoes, rapists or robberies, floods or fornication, suicides or tsunamis, divorce or death. We will be overwhelmed with the radiance and glory of God, and everything, including you and me, will be perfectly restored.

A Promise

We are not just headed to a place, a person, and a possession; we are also headed to a place where all the promises of God will be consummately fulfilled. And the crux of the covenant, "He will be our God, and we will be His people" will be consummately realized. Think of every promise you have ever read in Scripture, and think of them all being perfectly fulfilled.

In the new city there will be no possibility of us ever sinning again. There will be no paradise lost. Christ, the second Adam, has secured a greater garden than that of Eden. It is not only paradise regained and restored; it is a paradise that can never be lost again.

A People

We are not just going to going to a place, a person, a possession, and promises consummately fulfilled; we are also going to a people. In the city that is to come, there will be a multitude of people from every tribe, tongue, and nation. We will worship the Lamb of God together, side by side. No longer will worship hours be the most segregated ones. People from every race will join together before Jesus Christ to sing praises to Him. These people groups will bring the glory and honor of the nations into the new city. Together we will not only worship but we will work together in resurrected bodies for the glory of God.

I don't know the specific circumstances you are facing today, but I know you are facing, or about to face, some kind of suffering, sin, or difficult service. It is our responsibility as we walk with one another, whether through weeping or rejoicing, to help each other remember the wonder of the truth that Jesus is building a place for us and will remain with us in that place forever. We need to let John's words ring in our hearts and minds as we continue to look with eyes of faith to Jesus Christ and the city that is to come:

> And there shall be no more curse, but the throne of God and of the Lamb shall be in it, and His servants shall serve Him. They shall see His face, and His name shall be on their foreheads. There

shall be no night there: They need no lamp nor
light of the sun, for the Lord God gives them
light. And they shall reign forever and ever.
(Rev. 22:3–5)

Thinking It Through

- Jot down your present sin, suffering, and service in light of what you have learned about the
new heaven and the new earth in this chapter.

  Sin—

  Suffering—

  Service—

- How do you think of the new heaven and new
earth? How has this chapter confirmed your
thinking or challenged your thinking?

- In what area of your life is it difficult to keep
an eternal perspective right now? How has this
chapter encouraged you to fix your eyes on
Christ and eternity?

- Which verses in Revelation 22:3–5 particularly encourage you? Try to commit them to memory this week.

Bibliography

Clowney, Edmund P. *The Church*. Downers Grove, Ill.: IVP, 1995.

———. *Preaching Christ in All of Scripture*. Wheaton, Ill.: Crossway, 2003.

———. *The Unfolding Mystery: Discovering Christ in the Old Testament*. Phillipsburg, N.J.: P&R, 1988.

Currid, John D. *A Study Commentary on Deuteronomy*. EP Study Commentary. Webster, N.Y.: Evangelical Press, 2006.

Duguid, Iain. *Is Jesus in the Old Testament?* Phillipsburg, N.J.: P&R, 2013.

Emlet, Michael. *CrossTalk: Where Life and Scripture Meet*. Greensboro, N.C.: New Growth Press, 2009.

Frame, John. *The Doctrine of the Christian Life*. Phillipsburg, N.J.: P&R, 2008.

Golding, Peter. *Covenant Theology: The Key of Theology in Reformed Thought and Tradition*. Fern, Scotland: Christian Focus, 2004.

Ivill, Sarah. *1 Peter, 2 Peter, and Jude: Steadfast in the Faith*. Grand Rapids: Reformation Heritage Books, 2017.

———. *Hebrews: His Hope: The Anchor for Our Souls*.

Lawrenceville, Ga.: Christian Education and Publications, 2011.

——. *Judges and Ruth: There Is a Redeemer*. Phillipsburg, N.J.: P&R, 2014.

——. *Revelation: Let the One Who Is Thirsty Come*. Phillipsburg, N.J.: P&R, 2013.

Johnson, Dennis E. *Him We Proclaim: Preaching Christ from All the Scriptures*. Phillipsburg, N.J.: P&R, 2007.

Kleyn, Diana with Joel R. Beeke. *Reformation Heroes*. Grand Rapids: Reformation Heritage Books, 2007.

Lillback, Peter A., ed. *Seeing Christ in All of Scripture: Hermeneutics at Westminster Theological Seminary*. Philadelphia: Westminster Seminary Press, 2016.

Moo, Douglas. *The Epistle to the Romans*. The New International Commentary on the New Testament. Grand Rapids: Eerdmans, 1996.

Poythress, Vern S. *God-Centered Biblical Interpretation*. Phillipsburg, N.J.: P&R, 1999.

Robertson, O. Palmer. *The Christ of the Covenants*. Phillipsburg, N.J.: P&R, 1980.

Sproul, R. C. *What Is Reformed Theology? Understanding the Basics*. Grand Rapids: Baker, 1997.

Ten Boom, Corrie, John Sherrill, and Elizabeth Sherrill. *The Hiding Place*. New York: Bantam Books, 1971.